# PRAISE FOR SEEK

*Seek* is the perfect book for any woman who desires to get acquainted with God. Donna Jones leads women on an inspiring journey and does a beautiful job of weaving the practical, the biblical, and the personal in her introduction to God. Her refreshing and engaging style will leave you wanting to know Him more.

## Angela Bisignano, Ph.D.
Speaker and Consultant
Author, Beautifully Gifted: Equipping Today's Women for the High Calling of God

Donna is committed to honoring the people God has placed in her life—including you. *Seek* is solidly rooted in the timeless teaching of God's Word, and it is designed to put Christianity on the bottom shelf and answer questions you have always wanted to ask but couldn't. You are headed for a journey with the ultimate power to live the life you always wanted.

## Brett Eastman
President and Founder, Lifetogether Ministries

Donna Jones has captured the lofty concepts of the Christian faith and brought them down to where we live. Whether you are seeking the basics of the Bible, the practice of prayer, or the help of the Holy Spirit, this practical volume will enable you to better understand and consistently apply your faith. It is a powerful book that will quickly become your new go-to guide for seeking—and finding—a deep, meaningful life in Christ.

## Karen Ehman
Proverbs 31 Ministries Director of Speakers
Author of six books, including LET. IT. GO.: *How to Stop Running the Show and Start Walking in Faith*

I loved Donna the moment I met her, and I also loved this book the moment I picked it up. Packed within these pages is such crystal clear truth about who God is and how He woos and pursues His people! If you're thirsty to meet the *real* God who ministers to us in *real* ways, you're going to love this book too!

## Shannon Ethridge, M.A.
International Speaker
Bestselling Author, the *Every Woman's Battle series*

In *Seek*, Donna Jones tackles the question that we've all asked and, quite possibly, may be asking at this very moment: "God, who are You, really?" As she peels back the layers of curiosity and unveils the truth, she guides us into knowing more about the person of God, the selflessness of Christ, and the power and guidance of the Holy Spirit. If you're curious about God—if you're seeking to know Him more intimately—this book is for you.

## Jenifer Jernigan
Founder, Diving Deeper Ministries
Co-owner, Internet Café Devotions

Ironically, my best stuff for equipping men comes from what women reveal to me about their longings and frustrations in life. One thing women tell me is that broken female culture can be sincerely insincere—well meaning but often shallow, isolating and unsatisfying. Into this world drowning in synthetic connections and spiritual life comes Donna Jones. *Seek* is a coffeehouse connect in the midst of the gravities of life. If it were possible to *feel* a warm latte with a close friend, deeply connect, and be enriched with meaning through authentic dialogue, it is waiting for you in the pages of this book!

## Kenny Luck
Author, *Sleeping Giant*
Founder, Every Man Ministries
Men's Pastor, Saddleback Church, Lake Forest, California

This book delivers exactly what it promises—an intimate personalized introduction to God. In a wonderful blend of clear biblical truths and winsome personal stories, Donna Jones weaves a delightfully engaging encounter with our living Lord. The well-balanced blend of Donna's wisdom and investigative biblical studies provides a wonderful journey for any woman who would like to get to know God—and it is a powerful refresher for any woman who would like to deepen and enrich her faith. I encourage you to pick up this book and dive in. Your life will never be the same.

## Milan Yerkovich
Marriage Counselor, Relationship 180
Author, *How We Love* and *How We Love Our Kids*
Co-host, *New Life Live*

As a women's ministry director, I know firsthand the importance of having resources for *all* women in your church. Sadly, not much has been available for the new believer or the woman with questions about God—until now. *Seek* is the "must have" book for women who are just beginning their spiritual journey or those who want to make sure they're grounded in the basics. It is filled with insights and inspiration for any woman who wants to know and experience God in her everyday life. I love this book!

## Lori Marshall
Women's Ministries Director, Crossline Community Church
Laguna Hills, California

Wouldn't you want an intimate and inspirational relationship with the living God? *Seek* is the key to finding your deeper relationship with God. Donna Jones has truly unlocked the door to the riches of God's relationship storeroom!

## Dr. Carl Moeller
President/CEO, Open Doors USA

*Is God real? Can I know Him? Can He really be my friend? What do I do with the Bible? How do I pray?* Are those questions you've asked? In her down-to-earth, girlfriend-next-door style, Donna Jones walks with you and gives you direction and honest answers in your faith journey. Seek. Read. Find. There's so much to discover as you grow to know the God you're looking for.

## Jill Savage
CEO, Hearts at Home
Author, *Real Moms . . . Real Jesus*

Reading *Seek* is like sitting down with a close girlfriend while she lays out a plan and purpose for having a genuine, growing relationship with Jesus. Donna's conversational style will capture you as she dispels confusion about familiar Christian terminology. She gives practical, biblical advice to women on how to begin and continue in a lifelong relationship with Jesus. As the director of women's ministries in my local church, *Seek* is the book I've been searching for.

## Vicki Tiede
Speaker and Bible Teacher
Author, *When Your Husband Is Addicted to Pornography: Healing for Your Wounded Heart*

I love this book by Donna that helps us understand the basic fundamentals of the Christian faith. She is genuine and charming, and the book is an enjoyable read. It would be the perfect book for a women's small group.

# Chad Young

Author, *Authenticity: Real Faith in a Phony, Superficial World*

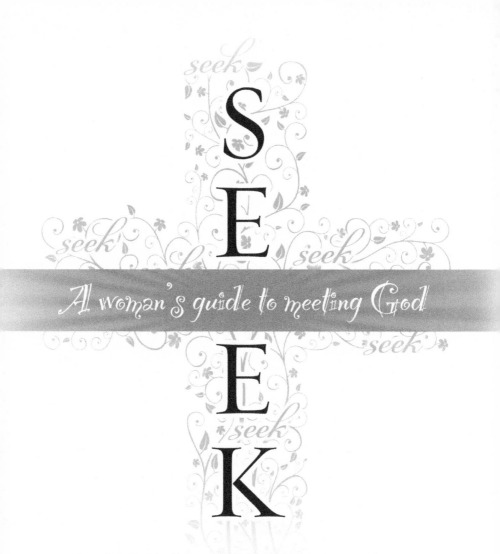

**S**

**E**

*A woman's guide to meeting God*

**E**

**K**

*Basic Beliefs of the Christian Faith for the Spiritually–Minded Woman*

# DONNA JONES

## Revell

a division of Baker Publishing Group
Grand Rapids, Michigan

© 2012 by Donna Jones

Published by Revell
a division of Baker Publishing Group
PO Box 6287, Grand Rapids, MI 49516-6287
www.revellbooks.com

Revell edition published 2015
ISBN 978-0-8007-2532-7

Previously published by Regal Books

Printed in the United States of America

Library of Congress Control Number: 2014958491

15  16  17  18  19  20  21      7  6  5  4  3  2  1

# S
# E
# E
# K

*To JP*
*Watching you live your life has taught me more about*
*seeking God than a lifetime of books could tell.*
*I love you.*

# Contents

# Acknowledgments

As every writer knows, no book is really the work of just one person. It takes a village. I would like to thank my personal tribe of friends and family who loved me, prayed for me and encouraged me to seek hard after God and his plan for my life. Without them, this book might never have been written.

To my husband, best friend and partner in life, JP: thank you for modeling what seeking God is really all about. If the mark of a Christian is love, you are the real deal in every way. Plus, I'm the only woman I know who can ask her husband virtually any Bible question and he'll know the answer on the spot. You were my Google long before Google was invented. I am blessed.

Taylor, Kylie and Ashton, my three precious children: thank you for allowing me to use your life stories as springboards for explaining how a great God works in the lives of ordinary people like us. Words can't even express how much I love you.

My heartfelt thanks go out to my wonderful friends at Crossline Community Church who prayed over this work every step of the way. You are the authors of this book as much as I am. A special thanks to Lori Marshall, my dear friend and partner in ministry, who gave me a deadline and made me stick to it; to Jean E. Jones, for reading my rough drafts and correcting my computer blunders; and to Alicia Hilton, who helped me facilitate the Bible study portion of this book, testing and refining as we went.

Kim Bangs and the folks at Regal Books have been cheerleaders for this project from the beginning. I am honored to work with you and to call you friends.

Finally, I want to thank my mom and dad, Don and Carol Riley, the original two who decided to seek God in our family. Because you decided to seek God, so did I. How could words express my thanks for a lifetime of love, support, encouragement and prayer? You make life fun.

# Introduction

What if you could meet God?

Would you want to?

These are pretty heady questions, to be sure, but most people give at least a casual thought to questions about God at some point in their lives. If you're reading this book, I'm guessing you're one of them.

I was too, once.

The summer I turned 10, our family took a road trip across the southwestern part of the United States. We cruised the highway in our Country Squire station wagon, complete with fake wood trim siding. It was the mid 1970s, and in our bell-bottom jeans, we were the picture of a typical American middle-class family. Think Chevy Chase's *Vacation* meets *The Wonder Years* and you've got the picture.

One evening stands out from all the others. My brother and sister slept soundly in the fold-down third-row seat, while I occupied the middle. I was bored with our long road trip, tired of reading and sick of endless card games. Instead, I wanted an earful of my parents' conversation. Leaning forward, I perched my chin on my hands, which rested on the back of the front seat. Before us sprawled colors of orange and pink and blue that filled the windshield from side to side with an array of vivid shades—one of the most breathtaking sunsets I have ever seen. We sat in silence, soaking up the beauty. Finally, Mom turned to Dad and whispered her private thought: "How can anyone doubt there's a God when they see something as magnificent as that?"

To this day I remember my immediate thought as clearly as I remember that breathtaking sunset.

*I doubt it.*

My mother's innocent comment sent me on a journey of uncertainty. I questioned everything I had ever been taught. *How can she be so sure? How can anyone really know if God is real?* My parents had no idea these thoughts rattled around in my brain, haunting me with fears that perhaps no one could really know with certainty. My disbelief felt liberating and debilitating at the same time. I was free to decide what I believed about God for myself, but I was unclear about just what that meant. It was as if the safety net of faith had been jerked out from under me with one swift yank.

I was left with only one thing I knew for sure: What I believed about God was a personal issue that no one could decide but me.

Though my doubts left me feeling a little bit like a leaf adrift on open sea, eventually those same doubts propelled me to ask questions. My questions motivated me to seek answers from people I figured knew more about God than I did. My family attended church, so I began listening—*really* listening—for the first time, to see if what my pastor and teachers said made sense. I remember timidly raising my hand during one Sunday School lesson when the teacher's explanation left me confused, and I can still picture the mixed facial expressions of my peers—some clearly glad that I had asked the question, and others looking at me as if I had two heads.

One afternoon, I snuck an old family Bible from the bookcase and began reading it alone in bed at night, although, to be honest, much of it seemed as understandable as Chinese at the time. I tried to be subtle in my faith quest so that no matter which way I landed on the God issue, no one but me would know—at least until I made up my mind. I wanted to explore God on my own terms, in my own way. But my heart sensed a tug I couldn't deny. If God was real, I wanted to know Him.

What I learned during my period of doubts, questions and seeking answers radically changed my life. Slowly but surely, I came to know God.

Over the years, I've come to realize that my journey isn't unique. Though the details vary, the same story can be told by millions of women all over the globe—women like you and me—whose questions and, yes, even doubts about God launched them into a season of curiosity. Curious women want answers.

Maybe you can relate. Maybe believing in God hasn't always been so easy for you either. Maybe you have doubts and questions. Perhaps you even feel a bit guilty about it. Don't. I know from firsthand experience that questions are good when they are asked from an honest, seeking heart.

Unfortunately, sometimes finding the answers we seek isn't easy, as my friend Kay knows all too well.

One spring afternoon, her dentist husband walked through their front door early from work with an announcement he couldn't contain: "I've become a Christian, and I want you to become one too." This struck Kay as a bit odd since she had been raised in a religious home as a child. *What's he talking about? I'm already a Christian.* What had happened to her husband? She rolled her eyes. His newfound faith sounded over the top and, to be candid, kind of wacko.

Determined to figure out the changes in her husband (which weren't altogether bad, she had to admit) she found a local women's Bible study and signed up. Hesitantly, she walked through the door, found her group and sat down. The women didn't look so odd. Pretty much like her, in fact. She felt relieved—for about two nanoseconds. Once the Bible study began, the women used religious words Kay had never heard. Clearly, they all knew what the others meant. Why didn't she? When they opened their Bibles, they flipped to the verses with ease.

Kay didn't have a clue where any of the passages could be found. Feeling out of place and uncomfortable, Kay couldn't wait for the study to end. The morning had been a disaster. Kay walked out the door and never looked back ... until the next September.

Hesitantly, Kay decided to give the Bible study a second try, but the whole episode repeated itself once again, leaving her feeling defeated, embarrassed and a little mad. Kay *wanted* to find a place where she could learn about her husband's newfound faith. Why was it so difficult? The Bible study women knew the lingo and had the spiritual stuff down pat. It was almost as if they belonged to some sort of private, members-only club.

Kay was an educated woman, but her lack of knowledge compared with the other women in the Bible study made her feel like an idiot. It reminded her of the "junior high" feelings a woman gets when she senses there's an "in" group and an "out" group, and she's definitely in the latter. Why was finding out about God so hard? Wasn't there a place for beginners? A place where someone would be kind enough to pull her aside and get her up to speed on the Christian basics? A place where she could ask her questions without being made to feel inadequate? There seemed to be plenty of information for women who already possessed a wealth of spiritual information, but what about women like her? And she knew more than most of her friends knew!

Kay went back to that same Bible study a third year (yeah, I know, I think she's a bit of a glutton for pain, too). But this time she stayed, determined to stick it out, no matter what. It was humbling and it was hard. But in the end, it was worth it. Like me, slowly but surely Kay met God.

Kay never forgot the feelings she experienced that first day of Bible study. She never wanted another woman who simply had questions about God to feel like she had felt. It haunted her until one day she sat down and wrote a Bible study for women new to the Bible, or who wanted to revisit the basics. She called the study *Essentials,* and it serves as the inspiration behind this book.

For years I had the privilege of teaching *Essentials.* When we launched the study, to be frank, we wondered if anyone would come. The first year 75 women attended. The second year the number grew to 150. Soon the number of women reached nearly 300 and kept on growing. What prompted these women to carve out time during their busy weeks to find answers to their questions about God? The same thing that motivates you and me.

Somewhere in the recesses of our minds we wonder, *Is God real? Can I know Him? If so, how?*

Women of all ages, seasons of life and life circumstances are asking these questions. Less than 24 hours ago, I hung up the phone with one of these women. She's an acquaintance who called to ask, "How can I become God's friend?" I had never heard meeting God put quite that way, but when I heard it, I loved it. Meeting God is not about becoming religious, following a set of rituals and traditions, or even about having Bible knowledge. Meeting God is personal. It's a relationship. It's a friendship between two parties who know one another and love one another.

My new friend's question is a valid one: If meeting God means beginning a personal relationship with God, what's involved? What do we need to know? What do we need to believe? What do we need to do? How does this whole "God thing" work? The answers to these questions are found in the pages of this book.

Maybe you're pondering the same things.

Perhaps you believed in God once a long time ago, but lately you've been wondering if there's more to life than merely believing God is out there, somewhere. Could He be personal? Could you experience God in a deeper way? Is there more to having a relationship with God than enduring a stale Sunday School lesson or sermon that has no real application to your everyday life?

Or maybe you've never really thought about God until now. Church, religion, prayer were for other people. *Those* people. And you certainly haven't wanted to be one of them. You don't want to be weird, but something in you compels you to think that maybe God is real, and knowable.

Perhaps something or someone has prompted you to explore the adventure of meeting God. You've had a thought-provoking conversation or observed something compelling in the life of a believer, and it has left you hungry for more.

Maybe the potential of meeting God gives you a sense of hope, meaning and security. Or maybe it's a bit overwhelming. Perhaps it's confusing. You might even be skeptical.

Very likely, it's all of the above. If you're seeking to meet God, you can expect some conflicting emotions. It can be exciting, but it can also be confusing, intimidating or even downright scary.

Whatever your motivation, know this: God is real. He knows you, loves you and wants you to know Him. But you already suspect the possibility that these things are true. That's why you're holding this book in your hands.

In the following pages, we're going to explore the concept of meeting God. And we'll do it in a way that would make Kay smile. There will be no religious jargon. The explanations will be simple and to the point. You'll find lots of real-life stories that bring the biblical concepts into twenty-first century living color.

As we seek God together, I am going to be upfront with you. I'm not a theologian, although I had several theologians read this manuscript to make sure the content was doctrin-ally sound. This book isn't intended to convince you that God exists, although it might, if you don't believe it already. This book doesn't contain all there is to know about God. On the contrary, this book is just a taste. A start. An introduction. And you should know that this book is not about religion, but rather, a relationship with your Creator.

This book was written simply because I think every woman should have the chance to meet God if she wants to.

If you plan to do the companion Bible study located at the end of each chapter—which I *highly* recommend—you'll need a Bible. I suggest the Life Application Bible in either the *NIV* (*New International Version*) or the *NLT* (*New Living Translation*), primar-ily because these Bibles have footnotes at the bottom of the pages that explain verses that may be difficult to under-stand for those new to Bible study. But any Bible will do. Also, you'll notice that the books of the Bible are listed in order at the end of this book. If you are new to Bible study, this list will help you navigate your way through the pages of the Bible.

If you are not doing the companion Bible study, buy your-self a Bible anyway and start reading the Gospel of John (the fourth book of the New Testament), which is all about the life of Jesus. If you're ambitious, you can read the 21 chapters of John's Gospel in one evening. It's a must-read. Truly.

One thing is certain; if you seek God, you'll find Him. God promises as much: "You will seek me and find me when you seek me with all your heart" (Jer. 29:13). If you want to meet Him, you can. If you want to see Him, just look. He wants to be your friend.

If you are ready, I would like to introduce you to God.

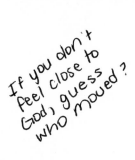

# Meeting God (for Real)

I encountered my first "stalker" at the age of six.

The culprit? Another first-grader, named Rob Cherry.

Rob, a shy, freckle-faced kid with hair as bright as his last name, followed me *everywhere*. Mrs. Lewis, our teacher, began each day with the same routine. One shrill screech of her whistle beckoned us into our single-file line outside Creeve Hall, elementary classroom number three.

As I raced across the blacktop wearing my super-cool Ked tennis shoes, I would find a spot in line only to discover Rob Cherry right behind me. Silently, we'd file into our cheery room, each child taking a seat on one of the dozens of little multicolored carpet squares placed in front of Mrs. Lewis's old wooden rocker. No matter which square I picked, Rob Cherry's carpet square mysteriously made its way next to mine.

When Mrs. Lewis excused us to our desks, Rob Cherry shadowed my path. Sometimes I'd glance up from working on a class assignment, only to find Rob Cherry staring at me adoringly. When he caught my eye, his smile would broaden into a wide grin, revealing two missing front teeth. At recess, when I chose the swing set, Rob did too. If I moved on to the monkey bars, so did Rob. And don't even get me started about what happened at the school cafeteria!

It didn't take long to figure out that, although Rob was too shy to say more than two sentences to me, he was more than just a little curious about getting to know me. In truth, his pursuit didn't bother me at all. Sometimes, I even found it a bit endearing—especially on one memorable occasion.

I had gone to the restroom. Because we were only six years old, our "potty" was located inside our classroom. As I sat with my scrawny little legs dangling over the toilet, too short to touch the floor, I turned to grab the toilet paper only to find an empty roll. *Uh oh.* But then I had a thought. *What if . . . ?*

"Rob?" I whispered, loud enough for someone standing outside the door to hear.

"Yes?" he replied weakly.

Rob was there! The kid even followed me to the toilet! At that moment, I loved him for it.

Perhaps you're wondering what this story has to do with meeting God. Oddly enough, a lot more than you might think.

Jesus had a Rob Cherry moment too.

The story, recorded for us in the Bible, is found in John 1 and is one of several recorded "first meetings" with God mentioned in the Bible. Every relationship with God starts somewhere—even for men and women who lived in biblical times.

## Curious People Seek

Three friends chat idly when, unexpectedly, Jesus walks by. One man—John the Baptist—knows Him. The others don't. Not yet. John can't contain his enthusiasm. Though he doesn't introduce his two friends to Jesus, he does tell them Jesus' credentials—He is the Messiah the Jews have waited for. On hearing this their eyebrows lift as they give one another a knowing glance. Curiosity piqued, they're eager for a closer look. So what do they do? They follow Jesus.

The two trail from a distance, hoping to see while not being seen. I can almost hear their conversation.

"Don't get too close; He'll realize we're following Him."

"Shhh . . . I'm trying to hear what He's saying. Can you make it out?"

"Do you think John could be right about Him? Could He really be the Messiah?"

"Do you think He knows we're watching Him? I hope He doesn't think we're stalkers."

The whole scene must have made Jesus grin. But instead of privately laughing at their feeble attempt to be inconspicuous, or becoming annoyed at two strangers who refuse to leave Him alone, Jesus stops. He turns, meets their gaze and asks only one question. "What do you want?" The men fumble for words, shuffle their feet and boldly blurt out, "Where are you staying?" I'm sure the moment the words left their lips they regretted them. *We have the Son of God standing in front of us and this is the best we could do?*

But for Jesus, it's enough.

"Come and you will see," He replies.

It was an intimate invitation. Inviting someone to come see where you live means offering a glimpse of the real you. An invitation to your home is an invitation to friendship. Jesus invited these two curious men to get to know Him personally, which is kind of mind-boggling when you think about it. Picture yourself running into a famous celebrity—one whose work you admire and whose stories you've read about in *People* magazine. How likely would it be for that person to ask you to spend the day with him or her? What are the odds that he or she would notice you following and say, "Hey, why don't you come over to my mansion in Beverly Hills and we'll hang out?"

But that's exactly what Jesus Christ did, though His accommodations were far from luxurious. In essence, Jesus said, "You've heard what others have to say about Me. Now I'm inviting you to come see for yourself."

Jesus doesn't offer a high-pressure sales pitch. He doesn't tell them to "get religion." He doesn't wave the guilt and shame card. He doesn't twist their arms. He simply asks a question—"What do you want?" and offers an invitation—"Come and see." Jesus welcomes people—all people—to explore the possibility of knowing Him.

---

> EVERY RELATIONSHIP HAS A STARTING POINT,
> EVEN A RELATIONSHIP WITH GOD.

---

The invitation Jesus offered to these two curious seekers remains as valid today as it was then. God *wants* you to know Him. Intimately. Personally. His invitation to "come and see" still stands. Let Jesus' words take the pressure off, but let them also motivate you to pursue Him further. Don't rely on secondhand knowledge of God. Some things in life are simply too important to sideline or delegate to others. You wouldn't ask someone else to be your stand-in at your wedding; you wouldn't hire someone to take your vacation; you wouldn't want someone to replace you at the birth of your baby. And you can't ask someone else to know God for you. We all must explore the possibility of meeting God for ourselves.

So start following even if only from a distance at first. Every relationship has a starting point, even a relationship with God.

But here's the mind-blowing part: Just when you think you're the one in pursuit of God, you begin to realize *He's* the one who's pursuing *you*.

Let's go back to the Rob Cherry story.

At first glance, the takeaway of this little incident—spiritually speaking—is that we should be more like Rob Cherry; we should be the ones who are so enamored with God that we pursue knowing Him. And that's correct. But there's more. God is like Rob Cherry too. Enamored with knowing us, He follows us everywhere. Consider what King David, the second king of Israel, wrote in Psalm 139. Read it slowly, thinking about the words and how they apply to you:

O LORD, you have examined my heart
    and know everything about me.
You know when I sit down or stand up.
    You know my thoughts even when I'm far away.
You see me when I travel
    and when I rest at home.
    You know everything I do.
You know what I am going to say
    even before I say it, LORD.
You go before me and follow me.
    You place your hand of blessing on my head.
Such knowledge is too wonderful for me,
    too great for me to understand!

I can never escape from your Spirit!
    I can never get away from your presence!
If I go up to heaven, you are there;
    if I go down to the grave, you are there.
If I ride the wings of the morning,
    if I dwell by the farthest oceans,
even there your hand will guide me,
    and your strength will support me.

I could ask the darkness to hide me
      and the light around me to become night—
      but even in darkness I cannot hide from you.
To you the night shines as bright as day.
      Darkness and light are the same to you.

You made all the delicate, inner parts of my body
      and knit me together in my mother's womb.
Thank you for making me so wonderfully complex!
      Your workmanship is marvelous—how well I know it.
You watched me as I was being formed in utter seclusion,
      as I was woven together in the dark of the womb.
You saw me before I was born.
      Every day of my life was recorded in your book.
Every moment was laid out
      before a single day had passed.

How precious are your thoughts about me, O God.
      They cannot be numbered!
I can't even count them;
      they outnumber the grains of sand!
And when I wake up,
      you are still with me! (Ps. 139:1-18, *NLT*)

Now that's a God who pursues! God is always with you, no matter how far away you roam. God knows every detail about you. He knows when you sit down. He knows when you stand up. He knows your private thoughts, your secret longings, your deepest hurts and your biggest fears. He's seen you laugh until you cry, and He's seen you cry from a heart so broken it seemed your tears would never stop. He was there when you were formed in secret. He knows about every day you have lived so far and every day you will live from this day on. He thinks about you all day. Every day. Talk about a God who is crazy about you!

But maybe you're thinking, *I wish I had the confidence in God the psalmist seemed to possess. If God would just make Himself obvious, I could find Him; I could believe in Him.* The thing is, God reveals Himself today just as surely as He did then. We just have to be able to recognize His presence in our lives.

---

DON'T RELY ON SECONDHAND KNOWLEDGE OF GOD. SOME THINGS IN LIFE ARE SIMPLY TOO IMPORTANT TO SIDELINE OR DELEGATE TO OTHERS.

---

Generally, God reveals Himself to seekers in one of two ways; the more obvious of the two is a dramatic, life-altering event. The sweet gal I mentioned in the introduction, who called asking, "How can I be God's friend?" experienced this type of event. Completely healthy her entire life, she woke up in the middle of the night to find she couldn't speak for a full 10 minutes. Doctors diagnosed her with a brain tumor. Within a matter of days she went from a vital picture of health to a patient in need of brain surgery. Life as she'd always known it had forever changed, and the experience grabbed her attention. Suddenly, eternity became a concrete reality rather than a theoretical "what if?" As a result, she met God.

More commonly, however, God reveals His presence and pursuit through events that some people like to call "coincidence," but in reality they are circumstances God orchestrates to draw your attention to Him. It's the conversation about God you overhear at Starbucks that somehow seems meant just for you. It's the co-worker who reads her Bible and isn't (totally) weird, but whose joy and sense of purpose you envy. It's the loving Christian family who moves in across the street just as your marriage and family are in need of repair. It's the believer who is enduring intense suffering but is filled with grace and peace. It's the teenager who decides to spend spring break serving the poor instead of partying with his friends. It's the unsolicited act of kindness you receive when life has gone from bad to worse. It's the seemingly random invitation to go to church or read a book—maybe even this one.

These ordinary yet uniquely orchestrated occurrences are meant for one purpose—to pique your curiosity just enough to explore the possibility of meeting God. When you tune into the circumstances of your life, you'll become aware of God's presence with you and His pursuit of you. As you sense God working in your life, take note. Don't chalk it up to "coincidence." Realize it for what it is—a circumstance in which the God of the universe has reached out to you.

Yes, indeed, God is a God who pursues.

Many women, however, struggle with believing God's relentless love could be true, largely due to a barrier of guilt and shame. *How could God love and accept me after all I've done?* We try to hide from God as a defense mechanism to cover our past mistakes and secret sins, resulting in one of two polar responses: We either avoid God completely or we set out to clean ourselves up before meeting Him. Women who choose the first response are thinking, *God demands too much, so I want nothing to do with Him.* Women who lean toward the second response reason, *If I can just get my act together, then I can meet God.* The trouble is, if we perceive God as a demanding tyrant or an uncaring sovereign, we will never seek Him. On the other hand, if we try to clean up our act before approaching God, we become burdened by religious dos and don'ts, which we can never quite achieve, so we continue to hide from God.

Often we harbor secret and not-so-secret choices that weigh down our burdened souls, leaving us to question, *How could God possibly want a friendship with someone like me?* If you've ever wrestled with thoughts like this, you're not the first. The woman known simply as the "Samaritan Woman" struggled with these issues too. Her story, found in John 4, gives us a peek into another "first meeting" with God.

## The Divorcée and the Divine

It had been a long day. Jesus was tired, worn-out and thirsty. All He really wanted was a place to rest His weary body. He spied a well in the distance, sat down beside the cool brick and shut His eyes for the briefest of moments. A woman approached—alone. It was an odd time to come to the well and even odder still for a woman to come by herself, but Jesus was glad that she was there. He asked her for a drink. Seems like a simple enough request to us, but not to her. She understood the implication of His question. In the ancient Middle East, men did not speak to women, since women were viewed as inferior, second-class citizens. Further, Jews never associated with Samaritans, who were considered despicable half-breeds. For Jesus to initiate a conversation with a Samaritan was shocking enough; but for Jesus to speak to a Samaritan woman? Unheard of.

But God is never bound by the prejudices of race or gender.

Warily, she gave Him a drink of water, and their conversation continued. He was unlike the other men she knew. He was kind and wise. He didn't seem to have an ulterior motive. As they chatted, it became apparent that Jesus knew every detail of her life though she had never seen Him before this moment. She was surprised to learn that He knew she was not married, but she had been. Five times. And if five shattered marriages weren't enough drama for one lifetime, the man she now lived with wasn't her husband.

Imagine the stigma of being a five-time divorcée and a live-in lover in a Middle Eastern culture, 2,000 years ago. Envision the sting of betrayal and rejection this woman endured in a society where marriage and motherhood were a woman's primary source of value and self-esteem. No wonder she traveled to the well alone. The women she once laughed with while dipping the day's water now laughed at her. Better to live in isolation than endure their whispers and gossip. But the women had nothing on the men. Her heart had been shattered into a million tiny pieces, not once, but five times over, and the man she currently lived with didn't even consider her worthy enough to put a ring on her finger. Truth be told, she didn't consider herself worthy enough, either. After all that she had endured, she wasn't a woman given to false illusion. Or hope. She was a woman with a reputation and a past that could make a truck driver blush.

But a broken life and a tainted history never dissuade Christ.

He offered her living water, the kind that springs up from inside a human soul. She wondered what He could possibly mean. *Who is this man who breaks social boundaries and cares more about my heart than my body? I'm a nobody. My life's a mess.* But she didn't want to appear ignorant, so she added her one piece of religious knowledge. "'I know that Messiah' (called Christ) 'is coming. When he comes, he will explain everything to us'" (John 4:25). Then Jesus declares, "I, the one speaking to you—I am he" (v. 26).

The woman who left her home to run an errand returned home having met God.

Just as Christ reached out to meet the woman at the well, God reaches out to you. Your background is irrelevant. Your past is unimportant. Your credentials—or lack of them—mean nothing. The compelling story of God is this: He bends low to be with us.

How? Sometimes God shows up in the most common ways. Far too many women assume that meeting God will be some sort of lightning-bolt experience. Although God manifests Himself in a variety of ways, according to the needs of a variety of people, most people meet God in the midst of commonplace, everyday life. They're invited to church, so they go and learn of God's love and forgiveness. The message is living water for their soul. They buy a Bible and start reading about the life of Christ. His words are living water for their soul. They have a conversation with a Christian friend and the chat is living water for their soul. Simple. Uncomplicated. Ordinary. But with a most extraordinary result.

## What God Wants

God wants a relationship with all people—those who seem to have life all figured out and those who don't. Those whose lives are going according to plan and those whose lives are falling apart; those whose lives are full of hope and those whose lives are filled with hopelessness. God wants to meet us all.

The question is not "Does God want to meet me?" The question you must ask is "Do I want to meet Him?" Whether or not you meet God depends on your response to Him.

When I was in college, I had a poster on my dorm room wall that read, "If you don't feel close to God, guess who moved?" The only reason any of us fail to know God is because we haven't taken the time to know Him. Maybe we haven't believed in His existence. Maybe we have been busy with other issues in life. Maybe we haven't wanted to know Him. Maybe we've thought that meeting God would make our lives a bore. Maybe we've felt guilty and ashamed. Maybe we've felt like He doesn't care. Or maybe we just haven't known how.

God wants you to know that a relationship with Him is possible. There's only one requirement: You have to want it.

God speaks these words through the prophet Jeremiah: "I know the plans I have for you . . . plans to prosper you and not to harm you, plans to give you hope and a future. Then you will call upon me and come and pray to me, and I will listen to you. You will seek me and find me when you seek me with all your heart" (Jer. 29:11-13).

The key to finding God is to seek Him.

IF YOU DON'T FEEL CLOSE TO GOD,
GUESS WHO MOVED?

God isn't playing a cosmic hide and seek game with you. You don't have to seek a God that doesn't want to be found. On the contrary, you seek a God who wants you to know Him and love Him. That's why Jesus came to earth. That's why God gave us His Word, the Bible. That's why God orchestrates circumstances, people and events to draw you to Him. Your background, your life experiences, your age, education, marital status, family history, health and circumstances—both good and bad—are not accidental. They are meant for a greater purpose. These things—and so many others—serve as catalysts for you to meet God.

You may have been running from God for years. You may have been ignoring God for decades. You may have been seeking God in a variety of unsatisfactory methods, rituals and religions. Whatever your past, this much is true: When you seek God, you will find Him if you seek Him with all your heart.

"What do you want?" Jesus asked the two curious followers. "Come and see," He offered. He's still asking the same question, and He's still offering the same invitation today.

Do you want to meet God? If so, perhaps it's time to start following God, even if only from a distance at first. He's already pursuing you.

When it comes to seeking a relationship with God, maybe we could all learn a thing or two from Rob Cherry.

# For Further Study

If you are doing this Bible study with a group, take a moment to introduce yourself and share about the day you met someone who later became significant in your life.

Becoming friends with someone is a fascinating phenomenon. One day you have no idea the person exists; the next day you do. Over the course of time, the person who was once a stranger becomes a friend. Such was the case with Jesus' earliest friends, or disciples, as they are referred to in the Bible. The story of their initial meeting with Jesus is recorded in John 1:10-50. They had no idea who Jesus was, but their friend John the Baptist did. So John the Baptist introduced them to Jesus.

John the Baptist was an interesting guy. He lived in the desert of Israel, where the story of Jesus takes place. He was a devout believer in God; he was a righteous man and a really good person. In fact, at the end of John the Baptist's life, Jesus proclaimed that there was no better man ever born than John the Baptist. That's some compliment!

John the Baptist was a preacher who taught people that the coming of the Messiah was close at hand. He preached repentance for the forgiveness of sins, and he baptized those who wanted to follow God wholeheartedly—thus the nickname, John the Baptizer, or Baptist. The Jews knew that God had promised a Messiah who would come to save their people. Devout Jews lived in anticipation of the coming of this Messiah. It's in this context that Jesus met five men who would later become five of His closest friends. Read John 1:19-50 and answer the following questions:

What did John the Baptist say about himself (see vv. 19-25)?

*He was a voice clearing a way for the Lord's coming.*

According to John the Baptist, who was to come after him? How does John describe this person (see vv. 26-27)?

*Not worthy to be His slave or untie His sandal*

The next day, John sees Jesus coming toward him. What does he say about Jesus (see v. 29)?

*Lamb of God who takes away the sins of the World*

To a Jew, the phrase "the Lamb of God" was a significant one. At Passover, a lamb was offered as a sacrifice for the sins of the people. Each family brought a lamb before the priest to be sacrificed as a substitute for their sins. Then the family would eat the Passover meal, including the lamb, in remembrance of God's deliverance of the Jews from slavery in Egypt during the time of Moses. The Passover meal served as a constant reminder of how God "passed over" the homes of those who had the blood of the lamb on their doorposts and spared them from death. The Passover meal ended with a reminder that the Messiah was soon to come. Passover is still celebrated by Jews all over the world today.

John continues his comments about Jesus in verses 32-34. What additional information about Jesus does John add (see vv. 32-34)?

*Holy spirit came down from Heaven + rested on Him + John Knew He was the Messiah*

No formal introductions to Jesus are made on this day. John merely describes Jesus in the way you or I might describe one friend to another. "Oh, that's Cathy, she's the most amazing cook!" or "Have you met Holly yet? She's the room mom" or "There's Julie, she's the vice president of her company." But the next day, everything changes. For the very first time, they meet Jesus. Read verses 35-39 and answer the following questions:

Imagine yourself in the two disciples' situation. You don't know Jesus yet, but you've heard incredible things about Him from someone you trust. What would you be feeling? Why would you be following Him? What is it that you would want from Jesus?

*Curiosity and excitement would make me want to follow / I'd have questions.*

Although we don't know for sure what the disciples were thinking, we do know they wanted to get to know Jesus better—up close and personal, if possible. What did they ask Jesus?

*Where are you staying*

What was Jesus' answer (see v. 39)?

*Come + See*

After spending the day with Jesus, what did Andrew conclude about Him (see vv. 40-41)?

*We have found the Messiah*

What did Andrew do in response to this conclusion (see vv. 41-42)?

*He brought Simon to meet Jesus*

Things move quickly now. Andrew and his companion are excited about meeting Jesus. Their excitement can't be contained. Jesus meets Philip, who comes to the same conclusion about Jesus that Andrew did. Philip finds his friend Nathanael and wants him to meet Jesus too.

Who does Philip say that Jesus is (see v. 45)?

> *We have found the one being talked about / son of Joseph from Nazareth*

How does Nathanael respond to Philip's assessment of Jesus (see v. 46)?

> *Can anything good from Nazareth?*

Nathanael met his friend Philip's enthusiasm about Jesus' identity with skepticism. Using today's lingo, Nathanael was basically saying, "Are you kidding me? No way. Have you gone off the deep end?"

I love Nathanael. He's a guy many of us can relate to. Our friends may be convinced about Jesus, but we're not so quick to believe. Like Nathanael, we need proof. I also love the way Philip responds to Nathanael's initial hesitancy. *Come and see,* Philip told him. *Come check Him out. Don't take my word for it. See for yourself.*

Can you remember the first time you heard about Jesus? What were the circumstances? What was your response?

> *Not sure ~ always grew up hearing about Him*

Upon meeting Jesus for the first time, Nathanael learns something that rocks his world. What is it? What does Jesus say about Nathanael (see vv. 47-48)? How does Nathanael respond (see v. 49)?

*Man of complete integrity / saw you under the fig tree*
*(49) You are the Son of God!*

Nathanael's initial skepticism turned to belief. What convinced him to change his view about Jesus?

*Jesus' knowledge about him*

Write down one thing you learned from reading the account of Jesus' first meeting with men who would later become his closest friends. How can this insight help you as you seek to know God?

*He is loving + patient / wants us to be real with our questions + faith*

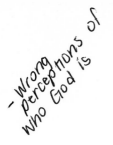

# 2

# The Father You Always Wanted

The first day I met my best friend, I judged her. She didn't know it at the time, but I took one look, heard one piece of information and pronounced a snap judgment—this woman and I will never be friends. Was I ever wrong! She was nothing like I had imagined.

Maybe you've had an experience like mine. Looks can be deceiving. So can too little information, or information from a biased source.

Too often we pronounce judgments about God without really knowing Him.

*God is out to zap me the minute I make one too many mistakes.*

*God is a cosmic killjoy.*

*God is too busy running the universe to care about my measly problems.*

*God wants me to get my act together before I come to Him.*

*God only listens to the super-religious person's prayers.*

*God grades us on the curve.*

*God is a figment of the imagination.*

Every one of us has conceptions and preconceptions about God. The key to meeting God is to allow yourself to explore Him as He is, not merely as you perceive Him to be.

One of the primary descriptions of God found in the Bible is *God the Father.* Depending on the quality of your relationship with your earthly father, this description either warms your heart or chills it.

Whether our paternal experience was ideal or sorely lacking, every one of us longs for a father who would protect us, provide for us, encourage us, guide us and care for us. We all want a daddy who loves his little girl.

The message of the Bible is that you do.

Too many women fail to see God as He is—a loving, caring, merciful heavenly Father—especially if their own father was anything but.

---

EVERY ONE OF US HAS CONCEPTIONS
AND PRECONCEPTIONS ABOUT GOD. THE KEY
TO MEETING GOD IS TO ALLOW YOURSELF TO
EXPLORE HIM AS HE IS, NOT MERELY AS
YOU PERCEIVE HIM TO BE.

---

As a 16-year-old newly licensed driver, I was anxious to get behind the wheel at every opportunity. My grandparents had just arrived from out of state, so when my mother asked someone to run to the grocery store for a gallon of milk, I eagerly volunteered and convinced my grandfather to ride along. We chatted as we drove. Did I have a boyfriend? How was school? Had I thought about college? Our idle banter went no deeper than the conversation fillers indicative of every adult-child exchange between people who know each other, but really don't.

Minutes later, we pulled into the parking lot where I steered my mom's brand-new family van into a parking space. I remembered the day my dad drove the car home, and Mom had been thrilled. I edged in carefully, but somewhere in the background I heard a faint, high-pitched noise.

"Honey, I think you'd better stop. I think you're hitting the car beside us."

My heart sank. How could I have hit the car? What would I tell my parents? My dad was going to kill me, for sure.

I sank back into the cushion of my mom's leather seat, trying to think. Trying to breathe. Adrenaline pulsed through my veins and I felt the racing of my own beating heart. After a few oppressive moments, we both left the van and examined the damage. There it was—a thin but obvious scratch that stretched from hood to bumper. My head dropped to my chest in utter humiliation.

"At least the other car isn't damaged," my grandfather offered hopefully.

There was nothing left to do but buy our milk, which weighed about as heavy as my heart. Side by side, we walked, Granddad and I, neither of us uttering a sound. My anxiety made conversation impossible.

We were standing in the checkout line when my grandfather turned to face me. "If you want to tell your parents that someone hit you, I'll go along with it," he whispered in my ear. I managed a weak smile but knew it wasn't an option. I was going to have to tell the truth and face the consequences.

We rode home in silence. Me in thought, Him confused about what to say to the distraught teenage granddaughter he barely knew. Finally, I pulled the damaged van into the driveway of our ranch style suburban home. I hesitated just a moment before willing myself into the house, each step feeling like a convicted criminal headed to the executioner's chair. Surely there would be raised voices. Disappointment. Grounded, for sure. Dread loomed over every detail of what was about to transpire.

I shuffled into the house, my eyes downcast and fixed on the shag carpet, which adorned every middle-class home during my teens. A few awkward moments passed. I sensed beads of sweat forming in my palms. My mouth felt dry and my tongue thick. Finally, I lifted my eyes, met my dad's gaze and confessed my crime. Dad leaned back in his recliner and sat silent for a few pensive moments before finally speaking.

"Well, I guess you've had your turn," he said thoughtfully.

"What do you mean?"

His faced warmed as he continued. "Everyone gets into an accident at least once in their life. Yours just happened sooner rather than later, and thankfully, it wasn't serious. I have only one question—did you learn from it?"

I could hardly believe my ears. No yelling? No punishment? Relief filled every fiber of my body. I hugged him tight.

A few hours later the phone rang. It was a girlfriend, inviting me to spend the evening at her house. *There's no way*, I thought. Not getting grounded was one thing, but being allowed to socialize after wrecking the family car was another. I was hesitant to even ask.

"I know I probably shouldn't even ask, and I know you'll probably say no, but Kathy called and wants me to go over to her house tonight—" I hadn't even finished the question before my father surprised me once again. Yes, I could go. Then I watched in disbelief as he reached into his pocket and handed me the car keys.

"Just be careful," he said, as a broad grin spread across his face.

What happened to me that day? It was more than just a car accident to be sure. I was the recipient of something the Bible calls mercy and grace.

Mercy is not getting something you do deserve. Grace is getting something you don't.

I had ruined the family car; my father had every right to discipline me. But he didn't. I deserved punishment; instead I got mercy. And if my father's mercy weren't enough, he gave me a gift I didn't deserve. He gave me his keys. He gave me grace.

You may be shaking your head, thinking to yourself, *That's great for you, Donna, but I don't have a father like that.*

Oh, but you do!

The Bible makes it clear that our heavenly Father is full of both grace and mercy toward us. Toward *you*. God shields you from punishment, if you will come to Him with an honest confession of your wrongdoing. But even more significant, He hands you the keys—not to the car, but to heaven itself. Talk about grace! That's the kind of Father we have.

The prophet Nehemiah recounted God's character when he proclaimed, "But in your great mercy you did not put an end to them or abandon them, for you are a gracious and merciful God" (Neh. 9:31). The God you seek isn't out to zap you over every wrong turn. He isn't vengeful toward those who come to Him. When we sincerely and humbly approach God, we don't get what we deserve. Instead, we get a gift that we don't deserve. We become the recipients of both mercy and grace.

The reality of God's grace and mercy is a gift we receive many times over. Each time we blow it but honestly admit our mistake, God extends His mercy and grace to us. Most women aren't used to this type of kindness. We're prone to live with guilt and shame, rather than in the freedom of love and acceptance. Guilt and shame cause us to hide from God, while accepting God's mercy and grace lifts the burden that guilt and shame produce, prompting us to want to run into His arms that are open wide with forgiveness and love.

On the fateful day I damaged the family car, my father extended mercy and grace. But in order for me to fully experience his mercy and grace, I had to accept them. Even though my father chose not to dole out punishment, I could have chosen to punish myself with thoughts of how stupid I was, or with acts of penance. I could have refused to accept his gift of grace by trying to earn his approval and love, rather than simply receiving it unconditionally. I could have abused his mercy and grace, taking them for granted, or responding with a sense of entitlement. I could have ignored his mercy and grace, failing to understand the gravity of what he offered so kindly. Each one of these actions would have influenced my relationship with my father. Not one of these reactions would have led to the love and gratitude I felt as a result of acknowledging and accepting his mercy and grace toward me.

MERCY IS NOT GETTING SOMETHING
YOU DO DESERVE. GRACE IS
GETTING SOMETHING YOU DON'T.

And so it is with our heavenly Father. When we approach God humbly and honestly, He lavishes us with His mercy and grace. When we allow ourselves to receive these good gifts, our appreciation and love for God grow. We begin to see God for who He is, rather than who we think He is.

## The Self-existent Creator

This merciful and grace-giving God is also the Almighty Creator. He created the heavens. He created the earth. He created human beings. And He created you. What does this tell us about our heavenly Father? Well, for starters, He's creative. The same God who painted the colors of a sunset also fashioned the intricacies of a human organ. With a word He created the complexities of the atom and the simplicity of an amoeba. He is the author of science and the basis for sociology. He made every star and every stargazer.

Because we were fashioned in God's likeness, we were designed as creators, as well. Some of us create through art, and some through the written word. Others create a loving family or successful business. Some find themselves most creative in the kitchen or the garden or the boardroom. We were designed to create because we were made in God's image. I supposed you could say, "like Father, like daughter."

The fact that God is the Almighty Creator also reveals His nature in other ways. He's powerful. He's in control. He's the author of life. He's infinite. He is the only true God.

In fact, when God revealed Himself to Moses and gave him the instruction to go free the people of Israel from bondage in Egypt, Moses had just one question: "Who will I say has sent me?" In essence, Moses asked God, who exactly are You? God's answer is fascinating:

> Moses said to God, "Suppose I go to the Israelites and say to them, 'The God of your fathers has sent me to you,' and they ask me, 'What is his name?' Then what shall I tell them?" God said to Moses, "I AM WHO I AM.' This is what you are to say to the Israelites: 'I AM has sent me to you'" (Exod. 3:13-14).

What did God mean?

When we introduce ourselves to people, we say things like, "I'm Donna, Kylie's mom" or "Hi, I'm Melissa, the new second-grade teacher" or "I'm Cassie. I'm in your biology class." In other words, we identify ourselves by position, relationship or function. I'm someone's wife or mom or sister or friend. I'm your co-worker, boss or client. I'm a neighbor or friend of a friend, and so on. In contrast, God doesn't identify Himself primarily by His position or relationship or function. He doesn't have to, because He IS. In other words, God is the self-existent one. His existence doesn't depend on someone else's existence, like our existence does. I exist because my mother and father existed and created me. I am, because they were. God just is. No one and nothing created Him. That's why He introduces Himself as "I AM." Period.

It's a mind-boggling thought. But would you expect God to be anything less?

If all this seems too much to comprehend, that's because it is. If you could completely understand God, He wouldn't be God—you would. And although some religions assert that we are gods, our own fallibilities and weaknesses and shortcomings testify that we are not. I can barely create a chocolate soufflé, much less a particle of matter, a planet or an ocean. How about you?

## The Great Pursuer

Though God holds the universe in His hands, He bends down low enough to walk with us through our everyday journey of life. Stop and think about that for a moment. It's an awe-inspiring thought. God Himself expresses this truth:

> For this is what the high and exalted One says—
> He who lives forever, whose name is holy:
> I live in a high and holy place,
> but also with the one who is contrite and lowly in spirit,
> to revive the spirit of the lowly
> and to revive the heart of the contrite.

I will not accuse them forever,
    nor will I always be angry,
for then they would faint away because of me—
    the very people I have created (Isa. 57:15-16).

God, the high and exalted one, lives also with those of us who are contrite and lowly—or humble—in spirit. What a beautiful picture of God's exalted, divine nature coupled with His love, mercy and grace.

God is high above us, yet He bends low to be with us. God is infinite, yet personal. God is holy, yet merciful. God is righteous, yet full of grace. God is all-knowing, yet He wants us to know Him.

Don't skim over this point. *God wants us to know Him.* The only reason we can know God is because He has revealed Himself in order to be known. He pursues us. He pursues *you.*

Before I was married, I wanted nothing more than to be pursued. I'd lay on my lime-green bedspread, crank up The Eagles as loud as my parents would allow and let my thoughts wander. Inevitably, I'd find myself daydreaming about how a cute boy in class just couldn't live without me. Or how I would meet Mr. Right and he would know immediately that I was "the one."

Sometimes the fantasies featured me as the friend who becomes the lover because of my irresistible charm. Yes, indeed, I wanted to be wanted. And not just by anyone, but by someone special. Sure, my college buddies and I dreamed of fulfilling careers and all that comes with "the good life." But deep in our hearts, we all shared an unspoken longing. We wanted to be pursued and wooed. We wanted to be loved. The need to be wanted is embedded in each of our souls. The good news is this: You are wanted. God pursues you with an everlasting love (see Jer. 31:3).

In fact, this is the message of the Bible—God's love letter to you. From the beginning of time, God has pursued His people. Right now, God is pursuing you. Make no mistake about it; it's why you're holding this book in your hands.

## The One Who Will Never Leave You

God's love toward us can be seen in His tender care for us. Like a good father who sticks by us in our good times and bad, our heavenly Father will never leave us nor forsake us. That's good news for a generation of women who have been abandoned by their dads through divorce or neglect or overwork. God Himself declares His commitment to us: "God has said, 'Never will I leave you; never will I forsake you'" (Heb. 13:5).

Several years ago, our family made a mid-year move. Anyone who has had to negotiate the process of making new friends mid-term knows how difficult this can be. For our son, who was nine at the time, the transition was particularly difficult. Our move meant leaving the security of two best friends he had known since preschool. To make matters worse, while our home was under construction, we lived in an apartment miles from the kids' new school, making after-school play dates all but impossible.

One rainy afternoon, while my daughters and I busied ourselves making cookies, my eerily accurate mom radar sounded an alert. Something wasn't right. I left the girls and crept upstairs to find my son's bedroom door shut. Placing my ear against the door, I heard the faint sound of Taylor's sobbing. I tapped a knock, then cracked the door just enough to see my heartbroken son laying facedown on top of his bed, his head buried in his hands. He was crying with such sorrow his shoulders bobbed up and down in waves of tearful sobs. His rough-and-tumble blue jeans and bright red sweatshirt failed to conceal the fragile soul beneath.

"What's wrong, honey?" I said softly.

He turned over and wiped his tear-stained face with the back of his hands. "I hate it here, Mom! I miss Austin and Neal. I just want to go home."

Truthfully, so did I. But what do you tell a child when you can't make it better? How do you heal the hurt? How do you make the pain go away? I struggled with what to say next.

Just then I heard a cry from downstairs. "Mom, come quick! Emergency!" The girls' crisis couldn't have come at a worse moment. I hated to leave my grief-stricken child, but the safety of another child demanded it.

With the girls' crisis resolved, I headed back upstairs. The overcast sky outside mirrored the dark cloud hovering over my insides. *Lord, please help me know what to say.*

I reached Taylor's door only to find a completely different scene than the one I had left just minutes before. My son was laying face up this time. His boyish hands were laced behind his head, his feet crossed at the ankles, his eyes riveted on the ceiling. The tears were gone, replaced by a furrowed brow. Clearly, he was deep in thought. What could have caused the change in his wounded soul? Cautiously, I walked across the room, perched myself on the edge of his bed and waited for him to speak.

"Mom, while you've been gone, I've been thinking," he said with utter sincerity. He paused then said, "I've been thinking about Uncle Dean's song."

My brother-in-law, a children's musical artist, had just released a song titled "Never Alone" based on Psalm 139. There, in the sacred quiet of a rainy afternoon, in the hallowed walls of a child's room, my nine-year-old son sang me the song he'd been pondering. When he finished the last chorus, he stopped and looked into my eyes.

"Even though I feel all alone, I'm not. God is always with me."

Here is what my son sang to me that day:

*If I could soar the great unknown,*
*Or swim the deep, I'm not alone.*
*If I could zoom the galaxies,*
*Or sail away on foreign seas,*
*His hand will keep me close*
*And lead me home.*
*Never alone.*
*My heart is not my own.*
*Never alone.*
*My heart is where He's home.*

Now, I was the one with tear-filled eyes. My son understood the nature of God's goodness, His faithfulness and nearness, not just in general, but to him, specifically. Personally. *God Himself has said, "I will never leave you or forsake you."* Knowing the truth about God makes all the difference—not just in our beliefs, but also in our lives.

When life gets tough, our natural response is to doubt God's goodness and love. We can easily wonder if He has abandoned us. For many women who have been abandoned by a father or husband, abandonment issues send them directly into survival mode. *I don't need anyone, anyway.* Or they bludgeon themselves with thoughts of unworthiness, believing that *no one will ever truly love me.* When we sense that perhaps God has abandoned us, we can easily slip into this same thinking. Feelings, however, are not always indicative of the truth. My son *felt* alone on that rainy afternoon, but as he focused on the truth—that God never leaves us alone—his emotions got in step with reality. As his thoughts about God aligned with the truth about God, his emotions followed. Life change resulted.

That's the way it works. All of us have notions about God—some more accurate than others. As our ideas about God get in step with the truth about God, we find we can trust Him, love Him, honor Him and know Him. And we are changed.

God is our merciful and gracious Father. He's the Almighty Creator of the universe. He's all-wise and all-powerful. He is the great I AM. He is holy. He is love. He is always with you. And He wants His children to know and love Him for who He is.

What has been your perception of God up to this point? Has it been an accurate portrait of the truth, or a poor caricature of God's nature?

Who is God?

God is the Father you have always wanted.

## For Further Study

Can you relate to having any misgivings about God? If so, express your thoughts.

When I was younger, I felt God expected perfection. Thankfully, I now feel something totally diffrent

The most basic tenet of faith is that God exists. Look up the following passages and write down what each verse says about the existence of God:

Psalm 102:25-27

*Laid the foundation of the earth, which will fade, but He will remain forever*

Acts 17:24-25

*Created whole world; He gives life + breath to everything*

1 Timothy 1:17

*All honor + glory to God / eternal King / one who never dies / He alone is God*

Hebrews 11:6

*must believe God exists and that He rewards those who truly seek Him*

*Hebrews 11:1 Faith is the confidence that what we hope for will actually happen.*

In these verses, what impressed you about the existence of God?

*His power*

Some religions assert that there are many gods. What does God have to say about this notion?

Isaiah 43:10-11

*I alone am God / There has never been another God + never will be*

Isaiah 44:6

*He is the first + last / no other god*

People worship many "gods" and have done so since time began. According to the following verses, what types of "gods" do we substitute for the one, true God?

Deuteronomy 4:19

*Forces of Heaven (sky, sun, moon + stars)*

Romans 1:21-23

*idols that looked like other people + animals*

Colossians 2:8

*empty philosophies*

Revelation 3:17

*$*

Can you think of any other things we can substitute for God?

*Anything that takes a ton of our time + focus on the correct priorities*

We worship what we love. We love what we believe will bring us pleasure. That's why so many people worship money, status, fame, popularity, relationships or success. The masses seek these things, thinking, *If I only have enough money, status, fame or success, then I'll be happy. Then my heart will be full and satisfied.* The alluring factor is that these things do bring a measure of satisfaction—for a while. But the pleasure is fleeting. There's always one more job to land, one more dollar to make, one more deal to sign, one more thing to buy. Only God can fill the hole in every human heart.

How does God fill the deepest longings of our soul?

Psalm 23

*He is w/us always / He gives guidance + rest*

*Beautiful*

Psalm 73:23-26

*He holds our hand + is the strength of our ♡*

Read the following verses and note what they reveal about God's character (or attributes, as they are sometimes called).

Deuteronomy 7:9

*Faithful + gives unfailing love to those who love Him.*

1 Samuel 2:2-3

*No one like Him / all knowing*

Nehemiah 9:31

Gracious + merciful

Psalm 90:2

God before the beginning

Psalm 106:1

He is good + faithful love endures forever

Psalm 145:18

Close to all who call on Him

Jeremiah 9:23-24

Demonstrates unfailing love + brings justice + righteousness to the world

John 4:24

Spirit

Romans 2:11

He does not show favoritism

2 Peter 3:9

*Patient + wants all to be saved*

1 John 1:5 (*Note*: There are four books written by John—the Gospel of John, which is the fourth book of the New Testament, and 1, 2 and 3 John, which are located near the end of the New Testament, just before Revelation. This passage references 1 John, the book toward the end of the Bible.)

*He is light ☺*

1 John 4:16

*God is love ♥*

Write down any new truths you have learned about God and His character from these verses. If you are in a group setting, discuss your insights.

Which of these attributes do you find most encouraging? Why?

*Unfailing love / holds our hand + Strength of our heart*

# 3

# God in Skin 🌿

I'm going to make this simple: Jesus is God with skin on.

In Jesus, we get a glimpse of God in the flesh. We see how He treated people. We get a peek into His priorities. We hear His teaching and gain insight from His words. We learn how to live, what to value and how to know God. Jesus shows us the way. Jesus *is* the way.

Born in an obscure village, to working-class Jewish parents, more than 2,000 years ago, His life marked mankind for all time. A carpenter by trade, Jesus began His public ministry at the age of 30 and was crucified a mere three years later.

Three years. That's 36 months . . . 1,095 days.

And the world has never been the same.

So how did Jesus' life begin?

From a human vantage point, Jesus' story began in Na-za-reth, a small out-of-the-way village in Israel. Nine months before his birth, his mother, Mary, received an angelic announcement: Though she was a young, unmarried virgin, she would become pregnant and give birth to the Son of God through a miraculous work of the Holy Spirit. When her fiancé, Joseph, learned of her pregnancy, he quickly made plans to end the engagement—he knew without a doubt that the child conceived in Mary's womb was not his. But an angel appeared to him, as well, instructing him to take Mary as his wife. This was to be no ordinary child.

Just days before Mary's due date, the Roman government announced a census that required all residents to travel to their ancestral hometown to be counted. Nine months into her pregnancy, Mary and Joseph made the grueling trip from their home to an even more remote village called Bethlehem. Bump by uncomfortable bump, they journeyed over the unpaved ancient roadway, the heaviness of Mary's belly and the child she carried weighing on both their minds and on her body. They didn't make the trip alone. Hundreds of others traveled, too, all headed to their ancestral homes at the same time for the same purpose. The foot traffic probably resembled our modern highways the night before Thanksgiving. Virtually everyone was going somewhere.

Mary and Joseph traveled slowly. In her condition, caution was of the utmost concern. They watched as friends, acquaintances and nameless faces in the crowd passed them by. The journey would feel exhausting by anyone's standards, but for a woman nine months into her pregnancy, the trip took an extra toll. Finally, Bethlehem was in sight. Relief flooded their weary bodies, but the relief was short-lived; all the inns were full with travelers who had made better time than the young man and his pregnant wife.

One innkeeper, however, took pity on their bleak plight. The sight of Mary's bulging middle and her husband's anxious concern over her condition made turning them away next to impossible—at least for someone with half a heart. He didn't have a room to rent, but he could offer them his stable where the more fortunate travelers housed their animals, if they couldn't find a better option. They looked at each other and sighed a breath of resignation. There were no better options. It would have to do.

Hours later, the contractions begin. The smell of their room-mates stifles Mary's need to breathe in big, labor-sized gulps of air. Joseph holds her hand, wipes her brow and remembers God's promise to them both. Their smooth, unblemished faces reveal a hint of their youth and innocence. Their eyes meet as if to say what the other knows—this is unfamiliar territory. But somehow they sense they aren't alone, and they are oddly at peace.

Finally, it was time. There, in the midst of an obscure vil-lage, in an obscure dwelling, to an obscure young couple, Jesus Christ was born.

With a beginning as humble as this one, and a life that spanned only three decades, how did Jesus change the world? After all, He was born before the Internet, cell phones and air travel. Jesus was even born before the printing press! The an-swer is revealed in His nature—fully human, yet fully divine. Only God in the flesh could pull off a feat as incredible as this.

From a human vantage point, Jesus' life began in Bethle-hem. From a divine vantage point, His existence is eternal. "In the beginning was the Word," the Bible tells us, "and the Word was with God, and the Word was God. . . . The Word became flesh and made his dwelling among us" (John 1:1,14). In other words, Jesus was God with skin on.

In Jesus' 36 months of public ministry, He healed the sick, taught the crowds and confounded the religious elite. No per-son, no matter how obscure or outcast, was unimportant to Je-sus. When He saw people, He *saw* people. And He valued each and every one.

## Jesus, the Compassionate Healer

As Jesus travels down a dusty road crowded with onlookers hop-ing to get a glimpse of the one who's stunned masses with His miracles, the town is abuzz. In the distance, Jesus hears what seems to be someone yelling at the top of his lungs, though what he's saying, Jesus can't quite make out amidst the hubbub of the crowd. Those closer to the action know what's being said and who's saying it. "Shhh, be quiet. You're obnoxious," they reprimand the blind beggar sitting by the road. But he's undeterred.

"Jesus, son of David, have mercy on me!" he pleads as loudly as his voice will allow.

He's an embarrassment, a social outcast. People roll their eyes and give him nasty looks, though his blind eyes can't see their distaste. He's one of *those* people the world pretends to pity but actually disdains. Though we might judge the onlookers in the crowd that day, I have to admit that maybe I would have responded the same way. Think about the scene. This was a street person—certainly not someone dressed in the finest or cleanest of clothes, and yelling with all his strength. I might think he was crazy, too.

Only one person in the crowd considers him worth giving the time of day.

Jesus calls for the man to come to Him. Don't miss what's going on here. Hundreds line the street, but only one receives a personal invitation from Jesus—the one who has the guts and the humility to ask for mercy. His social position is irrelevant. His physical condition makes no difference. Jesus sees beyond the externals to his heart.

Onlookers help the blind beggar get up and guide him toward Jesus.

"What do you want me to do for you?" Jesus asks.

"Lord, I want to see."

Moved with compassion and impressed by his faith, Jesus heals the blind beggar. For the first time ever, the man could see. And what a sight to behold—God with skin on standing right in front of him! Immediately he followed Jesus, praising God for what He had done (see Luke 18:35-42).

---

SOMETIMES IT'S THE THINGS WE DO
WHEN WE ARE DESPERATE
THAT MAKE ALL THE DIFFERENCE.

---

Don't miss the paradox. Filled with a heart full of empathy and concern, the creator of heaven and earth paused to reach out to the lowliest among us, granting not only his physical sight, but his spiritual sight as well. "I want to see" had meaning beyond the blind beggar's greatest expectations. One bold move resulted in one pivotal moment with Jesus. From that instant on, everything changed. Everything.

The blind beggar wasn't the only one whose pursuit of Jesus took guts. Nor is his story unique in the sense that he received both physical and spiritual healing. Consider the story found in Mark 2.

## Jesus, the Forgiver

Word has spread—Jesus is able to perform miracles. This news is of particular interest to one man and four of his friends—the man is paralyzed and has been for years. Admittedly, healing someone whose spinal cord is severed and whose muscles have atrophied would be nothing short of, well, miraculous, but this little detail doesn't stop the four friends. They roll their buddy onto a mat, each pick up a corner and haul him down to see Jesus.

When they arrive at the home where Jesus is teaching and healing, they discover that everyone else in town had the same idea. Suffice it to say, if fire codes existed in Jesus' day, the whole gig would have been shut down in a nanosecond. As it is, people cram elbow to elbow, vying for every inch of space in order to be seen by Jesus.

This isn't going to be as easy as they had hoped.

But the four friends don't give up. They climb onto the roof, remove the tiles, cut a hole in the ceiling and lower their paralyzed friend smack dab in front of Jesus. One of the things I plan on asking Jesus when I get to heaven is if this whole scene made Him laugh. Honestly, it would be funny if the situation hadn't been so desperate.

But sometimes it's the things we do when we are desperate that make all the difference.

Jesus took one look at the man on the mat and declared, "Son, your sins are forgiven" (Mark 2:5).

Though the text doesn't record what the man thought at this point, it's a safe bet to assume this wasn't exactly the message he was hoping for. *Forgive my sins? Are you kidding me? How about healing my legs?*

But Jesus knows all things. He even knows the thoughts of the religious leaders present that night. He's aware of their skepticism and their criticism. *Who is this who claims to be able to forgive sins?* Only God can forgive sins. Surely this could be nothing short of blasphemy—unless of course, Jesus is God.

Jesus turns once again to the paralyzed man on the mat lying in front of Him. Looking into his face, Jesus has just one more thing to say to him, a rhetorical question. "Which is easier: to say to this paralyzed man, 'Your sins are forgiven,' or to say, 'Get up, take your mat and walk'? But I want you to know that the Son of Man has authority on earth to forgive sins.' So he said to the man, 'I tell you, get up, take your mat and go home'" (Mark 2:9-11).

To the amazement of the throngs of people there, the man did exactly that.

In that one act, Jesus demonstrated His authority to heal and to forgive—authority reserved for God alone. This was an important moment, a defining one: Jesus went public. He established His identity as God in the flesh with His words, and confirmed His identity as God in the flesh with His miracle. Jesus wanted there to be no doubt in regard to His character, His nature and His identity.

This story illustrates just one of the numerous occasions Jesus made His divinity clear. During His brief time on earth He healed the sick, fed the hungry, taught the eager and corrected the misguided. He performed miracles that were witnessed by hundreds and, sometimes, even thousands. Naturally, His following grew, stirring the jealous hearts of the religious establishment who resented His popularity. When challenged over His claims to be God's son, Jesus responded by pointing to His ability to do the miraculous. *If you don't believe because of my words, at least believe because of my works* was His logical contention. For those who sought the truth, Jesus left no doubt.

## I and the Father Are One

Jesus' claims were bold, to be sure . . . audacious, even. But His bold, audacious assertions were always backed up by bold, audacious actions. Still, His declarations stirred controversy, just as they do now. Most people aren't offended when you talk about God, but mention the name of Jesus, and watch them squirm. The very name incites a reaction—either for Him or against Him. No other religious figure stirs such deep emotions. People don't get bent out of shape over Buddha or Confucius or the gods of Hinduism. Ever wondered why?

Quite simply, it's because Jesus is unique. You may love Him or you may hate Him, but you can't stay neutral about Jesus. This has always been the case. Consider the conversation that Jesus had with the religious elite, who resented His widespread popularity:

> It was winter, and Jesus was in the temple courts walking in Solomon's Colonnade. The Jews who were there gathered around him, saying, "How long will you keep us in suspense? If you are the Messiah, tell us plainly."
>
> Jesus answered, "I did tell you, but you do not believe. The works I do in my Father's name testify about me, but you do not believe because you are not my sheep. My sheep listen to my voice; I know them, and they follow me. I give them eternal life, and they shall never perish; no one will snatch them out of my hand. My Father, who has given them to me, is greater than all; no one can snatch them out of my Father's hand. I and the Father are one."
>
> Again his Jewish opponents picked up stones to stone him, but Jesus said to them, "I have shown you many good works from the Father. For which of these do you stone me?"
>
> "We are not stoning you for any good work," they replied, "but for blasphemy, because you, a mere man, claim to be God" (John 10:22-33).

Some contend that Jesus never claimed to be God. Read the last sentence quoted above one more time. Why did the Jewish religious establishment want to stone Him? Because Jesus claimed to be God. Regarding Jesus' assertion to be God, C. S. Lewis wrote:

I am trying here to prevent anyone saying the really foolish thing that people often say about Him: "I'm ready to accept Jesus as a great moral teacher, but I don't accept His claim to be God." That is the one thing we must not say. A man who said the sort of things Jesus said would not be a great moral teacher. He would either be a lunatic—on a level with the man who says he is a poached egg—or else he would be the Devil of Hell. You must make your choice. Either this man was, and is, the Son of God: or else a madman or something worse. You can shut Him up for a fool, you can spit at Him and kill Him as a demon; or you can fall at His feet and call Him Lord and God. But let us not come with any patronizing nonsense about His being a great human teacher. He has not left that open to us. He did not intend to.[1]

Those who stood in the crowd listening to Jesus speak understood the audacious nature of Jesus' claim when He stated, "I and the Father are one." There was no mistaking what Jesus meant.

They just didn't like it.

The necessity of clarifying who He was and why He came to earth was always paramount in Jesus' mind. He wanted His followers to be certain about His identity and His purpose. He told them plainly that He was the Son of God and proved His assertion with numerous miracles they witnessed firsthand. He taught with authority. He lived His life as an example to follow. He predicted His own death. He rose from the grave. He left them no doubt.

Those who knew Jesus *knew* Jesus.

But not everyone believed Him then, just as not everyone believes Him now. Why not? Well, some were jealous, some were skeptical, some were disinterested and some were uninformed. But mostly, those who didn't believe understood that belief in the claims of Christ meant life change. You can't acknowledge that someone is God's Son but go about your life as if this fact means nothing. To admit that Jesus was and is the Messiah—the one prophesied in the Hebrew Scriptures (what we refer to as the Old Testament)—demands an allegiance to a greater power, a choice not everyone was willing to make.

Was there outside proof that confirmed Jesus' claim to be the Messiah, the Son of God? You bet. Jesus' life fulfilled more than 300 prophecies foretold hundreds of years before His birth, including where He would be born (Bethlehem), His virgin birth, where He would grow up (Nazareth) and the type of death He would die (crucifixion—a form of death penalty that hadn't even been invented when it was prophesied). If you want to read a few prophecies for yourself, check out the book of Isaiah and read Isaiah 7:14, 9:6, and chapter 53. Remember, these predictions were written *hundreds* of years before Jesus lived. From a purely mathematical standpoint, the likelihood that someone could fulfill just 8 of the more than 300 prophecies is 10 to the seventeenth power, or 1 in 100,000,000,000,000,000! Jesus fulfilled them all. This fact alone provides compelling evidence regarding Jesus' divine nature.

But sometimes it's more convenient to ignore proof than to submit to it.

My husband's father died when my husband was nine years old. His dad was diagnosed with lung cancer and fought a losing battle with the dreaded disease for more than two years. Though he had ample warning and even endured several extended hospital stays, he left his wife and three children alone and penniless. He had purchased no life insurance. He made no plan or provision for their care after his death.

My mother-in-law had neither a high school diploma nor a driver's license. In his healthier days, my husband's dad worked and his mom stayed home and cared for the kids. When the doctor's heartbreaking call came on a summer evening, she hung up the phone to face her new reality. She had no money, no education, no way to get to work—even if she could find it—and no husband. Though he was a good man who loved his family, JP's dad had difficulty (understandably) coming to terms with the inevitable.

Sometimes it seems easier to ignore the proof. "Seems" is the operative word. Eventually, the proof always catches up with us.

Purchasing life insurance, teaching his wife to drive the family car, helping her to secure employment, encouraging her to get her high school diploma—these things would have required an admission my husband's father simply wasn't willing to face. Perhaps he wanted to cling to hope. Perhaps he thought an admission would mean he had given up the fight for life. I can understand his actions. You probably can, too. Facing difficult truth can be, well . . . difficult.

Lest you think his response was unusual, just think about the denial that goes on every day in homes across America. *I'm not an alcoholic, I just drink to take the edge off; I'm not an addict, I could quit anytime; It's not wrong. Everyone does it. My spending isn't that bad; after all, I deserve a treat or two, don't I?*

Many of us can't face proof that is right in front of our faces, even if that proof has to do with God; perhaps especially if that proof has to do with God. The fact that some things are hard to accept doesn't make them untrue. Sadly, my husband's father never came to terms with the fact that his body was riddled with cancer, but his denial didn't make it any less real.

Jesus' claim to be the Son of God proved difficult for some to grasp. But life's most challenging truths are almost always the most difficult to digest. Jesus was born and He lived among us. He was fully human, but just as fully divine. Who else could calm a raging storm with a word? Who else could raise the dead with a touch? Who else could make a blind man see or a lame man walk or a woman with a hemorrhaging disease whole? Who else could heal a human heart from the sorrow of a broken life, dashed dreams, heartache or pain? Who else could change the course of human history and scores of human lives in only 36 months? Only God with skin on.

## Jesus, Our Savior

As Jesus taught crowds of people and healed them, His popularity spread. His message was refreshing, life giving and backed up by an authentic life. But His popularity incited religious jealousy. In the minds of the religious establishment, Jesus simply had to go. Too many people began following Him rather than them. So they came up with a plan—betrayal, a mock trial and false accusations that were never proven to be true, even by the admission of those who presided over the trial. These leaders incited riots, and the mobs demanded Jesus' death.

Through it all, Jesus said not a word. Though He had absolute power and could have stopped it in a single breath, He let it happen. All of it—all the beatings, the mocking words, the false accusations, the nails cruelly driven into the sensitive flesh that connects the wrist to the hand and the ankles to the feet.

He let them nail Him to a cross to die. He had to. It was the only way to pay for the sins of all mankind and satisfy God's holiness. It was the reason He came to live among us. Why did Jesus do it? One reason: love. "This is love: not that we loved God, but that he loved us and sent his Son as an atoning sacrifice for our sins. . . . And we have seen and testify that the Father has sent his Son to be the Savior of the world" (1 John 4:10,14).

On a lonely, dark Friday, God in the flesh willingly died for the sins of the whole world.

In a very real sense, Jesus' death saved us from ours. As I write these words, tornadoes ravage the southern United States. My aunt lives in Tennessee, where a tornado left a wake of death and devastation just days ago, killing one of her long-time co-workers. The man's son had crouched into a human ball, trying to protect himself from the tornado; the man's wife had placed her body on top of the boy's. In an effort to shield his wife and son from harm, the man laid his body on top of them both. But the powerful wind proved too much. The man's body was flung into the force of the tornado, but his selfless sacrifice saved his wife and child. Motivated by love, he willingly died so that they could live.

That's what Jesus did for us.

An innocent man, Jesus freely laid down his life for ours. God's body covered our sin. He willingly died so that we could live. That's the loving message of the cross.

## Jesus, the Resurrected Lord

After Jesus' death, His body was removed from the cross and laid in a tomb carved out of rock. A huge boulder sealed the opening, and a Roman guard was placed in front to secure the site from thieves.

Early on Sunday morning, three women came to pay their respects. Saturday had been the Passover Sabbath, or they would have come sooner. They were grief-stricken ever since they watched the awful, humiliating scene thrust on their Savior. If only they could push the imagery out of their minds: how His blood spewed out when the spikes were driven into His innocent hands and feet; how His body was torn by the barbaric beating with whips laced with fragments of glass; the crown of thorns thrust down upon His head, causing droplets of blood to mix with His sweat and sting His eyes. It was almost too much to watch. Their bloodshot eyes revealed the sorrow of the past three days.

But what was done was done; now they were thinking practically: *Who will move the boulder for us?* They knew they certainly didn't have the strength. When they arrived, they received the shock of their lives—the stone had been rolled away and the tomb was empty. Jesus had risen from the grave. Sin had been paid for. Death had been conquered.

You might think His followers readily accepted His resurrection. After all, hadn't they witnessed Him calm a storm with a word? Hadn't they been present when He turned water into wine, walked on water and healed the blind? Hadn't they heard Jesus' own proclamation that He was one with the Father?

But they didn't believe. Not at first. It just seemed like too big of a miracle. They had watched their Lord die. And who on earth could conquer death?

In fact, it wasn't until Jesus appeared to them after His resurrection that they truly believed. To confirm and reaffirm His resurrection, Jesus appeared to them over a period of 40 days, sometimes in small groups and, on one occasion, appearing to more than 500 people together.

But when they saw Him, they knew Him. They knew that all He had said and done and demonstrated were true, without a doubt. In fact, history tells us they staked their lives on it. All but one died a martyr's death because they would not renounce who they knew Jesus to be. The single disciple who wasn't martyred died in exile for his faith in Christ.

Why would these early followers of Jesus be willing to die for their belief in Him when it would have been so simple to save their lives? A single word by any one of them; one admission that perhaps Jesus was not who He claimed to be; a slight innuendo that maybe Jesus wasn't the saving Messiah after all; a tiny insinuation that the resurrection could have been a hoax; any one of these was all it would have taken to be set free. Surely, if they knew Jesus hadn't been resurrected, they wouldn't have staked their lives on it. If they had doubts about His character or claims or divinity, certainly one of them—if not all of them—would have called it quits. Yet, not one of His true followers recanted. Not one.

They knew what they knew. They knew *who* Jesus was and is. And because they knew, they believed.

Jesus is God with skin on.

## For Further Study

Look up the following Bible passages. What do these Scriptures tell you about the way Jesus viewed people? What do these passages tell you about the way Jesus treated people?

Matthew 9:36

Matthew 23:27

Mark 1:40-42

_____

_____

Luke 5:29-32

_____

_____

Luke 18:15-17

_____

_____

John 11:32-35

_____

_____

What do these verses tell you about how Jesus sees you?

_____

_____

_____

_____

Jesus was unique in the way He dealt with others. More importantly, Jesus was unique in Himself. The Bible makes it clear that Jesus is the unique God-man—perfectly God and perfectly man. Look up the following verses and write down the phrase that indicates Jesus' deity ("deity" is the nature or state of God):

John 12:44-46

_____

_____

_____

John 14:8-11

Colossians 1:15-19

Colossians 2:9

John 1 reveals Jesus' divine nature in a unique manner. Read John 1:1-3 and answer the following questions:

Who was "in the beginning"?

In the beginning, who was the Word with?

In the beginning, who was the Word?

Now look at John 1:14. What did the Word do? According to John 1:1-3 and 14, who is the Word?

Write down any new insight you have gained about Jesus' deity.

_____

_____

_____

Jesus is fully God. When the angel announced Jesus' birth, he said that Jesus would be called Immanuel, which means "God with us" (Matt. 1:23). But Jesus was also fully human. What do you learn about Jesus' humanity from the following verses?

Luke 2:41-51

_____

_____

Luke 2:52

_____

_____

John 11:35

_____

_____

Hebrews 4:15

_____

_____

What was unique about Jesus' human birth, according to Matthew 1:18-25?

_____

_____

_____

What was unique about His human character, according to 1 John 3:5?

_____

_____

According to John 3:16-17, why did Jesus come into the world?

_____

_____

Read the following verses and answer why Jesus died on the cross:

Isaiah 53:4-6

_____

_____

Mark 10:45

_____

_____

Romans 5:6-10

_____

_____

1 Corinthians 15:2-4

_____

_____

Jesus died a horrific death by crucifixion. Although He did no wrong, He willingly paid the price for all wrongs done by every human being throughout time. He sacrificed Himself for you and for me and for millions of others just like us. Jesus didn't merely come to earth to be an example or a religious leader or a teacher. Jesus came to earth to be our Savior. He came to set us free; to reconcile us to God; to wipe our sins off the face of the map. Because Jesus lived a sinless life, He was a just substitute for the sins of mankind, which makes His death unique. However, His death was also unique in another way.

Read the following passages and note what happened to Jesus after His death:

Mark 16:1-7

1 Corinthians 15:3-8

Were there eyewitnesses to Jesus' resurrection? If so, how many (at the least)?

Based on the following passages, what is the significance of Jesus' resurrection?

John 11:25-26

1 Corinthians 6:14

**Note**

1. C. S. Lewis, *Mere Christianity* (New York: Macmillan/Collier, 1955), n.p.

# 4

# The Invisible God

You can't live the Christian life on your own.

Does that surprise you?

Thousands of women try to live "a good Christian life," constantly failing and consistently plagued by guilt, asking themselves, *Why does the Christian life seem to work for everyone else, but not for me? Why do I still struggle with the same things over and over and over again?*

For some, these thoughts result in feelings of condemnation and shame. Others shrug their shoulders and wonder, *Why even try to live like a Christian?* Both responses lead to the same result—a life lived distant from God. So what's the solution? If the Christian life can't be lived on our own, who's available to help us? Can a pastor or a spiritual mentor? Both are certainly helpful, but they're only human. They have time constraints and responsibilities of their own. No matter how kindhearted or generous, they still can't be available 24/7. So who can help? Is there anyone?

Yes. It's the Holy Spirit.

The Holy Spirit was given to help us live the Christian life.

Which is a really good thing.

Several years ago, our family planned a camping trip with a group of dear friends. On paper the adventure sounded fun. Beach bonfires. Oceanview sunsets. I pictured myself lounging on the beach with a good book in my hand and my toes in the sand, while my children frolicked happily in the gentle ocean waves.

Our friends were upfront with us. They made it clear that it would be no luxury RV camping excursion. This was a pitch-a-tent-on-the-beach campout; but still, our friends made it sound exciting. The minute we pulled into our campsite, I knew this would be a l-o-o-o-n-g week. Yes, we had an ocean view—from high atop a dirt hill where the wind whipped our tent like Martha Stewart whips her meringue. One look at my three small children, and I quickly realized that filth, dust and sand could seep into more crevices than I thought humanly possible. With all the mess, cooking was a hassle. Sleeping was a hassle. Frankly, everything was a hassle.

And I had a crummy attitude.

Of course, I carefully concealed my stinky outlook. We were with friends, after all. So I put on a happy face and said all the right words. I tried to have a good attitude, I really did. But inside, my soul was twisted in about 50 different ways, none of them good. My attitude was making me miserable. Everyone else seemed to be taking the situation in stride. What was wrong with me? I decided I needed to go on a run, clear my head and get some perspective. As I jogged along the beach, I began praying. "Lord, what's the matter with me? I'm a mess."

And then I heard the faint little whisper. It was simply a reminder of God's truth. "The fruit of the Spirit is love . . ." (*Was I filled with love? No way . . .*) "and joy . . ." (*Well, that one was definitely missing . . .*) "and peace . . ." (*I was experiencing anything but peace*) "and patience." (*Are you kidding me?*) "What about kindness, goodness, faithfulness or self-control?" (*No, no, no and no.*)

No wonder I was miserable.

So what was the solution? Did I make a commitment to do better, grit my teeth and will myself into a positive attitude? I did not. I'd been trying that tactic all week with no success. Instead, I acknowledged my crummy attitude to God, asked for forgiveness and to experience the Holy Spirit's presence in my life. *God, I can't will my attitude into a good place, so I want to exchange my ways for Yours,* I prayed.

I finished my run and headed back to the filthy mess we called home for the week.

The tent was still a disaster. The kids still had dirt stains all over their faces and sand in their hair. The ground was still hard, and dust still whirled around our feet as we walked. Our food was dangerously close to becoming a health hazard, and my husband hadn't showered or shaved in days. But even in the midst of the chaos, my soul was at rest. No longer was I filled up with me. I was filled up with Him. When the Spirit fills our life, He produces His nature in ours.

Of course, not all changes are instantaneous. Like a toddler learning to walk, often our attempts at living the Christian life by the power God's Spirit are scattered with failure. Sometimes it's two steps forward, one step back. But in time, the Holy Spirit will change us as we yield to His direction.

The bottom line is this: We can never try hard enough to follow God or His ways and succeed without His help. Thankfully, God has given us His Spirit to enable us to follow Him. The Spirit was given to help us do what we can never do on our own.

## Jesus Explains the Holy Spirit

When Jesus Christ lived on earth, the human race experienced God in the flesh—God with us. But when He died and was resurrected, He didn't leave us alone, without God in the world.

The Holy Spirit was given so that God would still be with us, not in the flesh but in the Spirit. Scripture tells us that this is to our benefit (see John 16:7-11), because a person who lives in the flesh is constrained by the flesh. You can't be in Jerusalem and Rome at the same time, for instance. But the Spirit of God isn't limited by human flesh. He can be with believers in London, in Moscow, in Tokyo and in Los Angeles, all at the same time. Jesus on earth was God with us. The Holy Spirit is God in us.

Jesus explained this to His disciples during their conversation at the Last Supper, the night before His crucifixion. Jesus, of course, knew the event that would transpire the following day, but His followers didn't have a clue. In an effort to prepare them for the grueling days ahead, Jesus encouraged them with these words:

> If you love me, keep my commands. And I will ask the Father, and he will give you another advocate to help you and be with you forever—the Spirit of Truth. The world cannot accept him, because it neither sees him nor knows him. But you know him, for he lives with you and will be *in* you (John 14:15-17, emphasis added).

Prior to the cross, the Holy Spirit—sometimes referred to as "the Spirit of truth," "the Advocate," "the Comforter," "the Counselor" and "the Helper"—lived with God's people. After Jesus' death and resurrection, the Holy Spirit came to live *in* God's people. This truth would prove vital to those early disciples. Grieved after Jesus' death, they needed a comforter. Confused, they needed a counselor. Accused, they needed an advocate. Doubtful, they needed a truth-giver. Everything Jesus was to them, the Holy Spirit was *in* them.

Our needs are not so different from those early disciples. We need guidance, help, comfort and truth, just as they did. God, the Holy Spirit, is our helper, our advocate, our comforter and our guide. The Holy Spirit empowers us to follow God in our real, everyday lives.

---

JESUS WAS GOD WITH US;
THE HOLY SPIRIT IS GOD IN US.

---

## Allowing the Spirit to Work in Your Life

The Holy Spirit helps us follow God by helping us to understand God's Word and obey it. This means—and here's the best part—we don't have to try to follow God alone. God gives us the Holy Spirit to help us live the Christian life. The Holy Spirit reminds us how to follow God, but He does much more—He *enables* us to follow God. We don't have to live the Christian life depending on our own limited efforts to be "good Christian girls." Instead, the Holy Spirit's presence in our life provides the resources we need to walk with God. The Helper helps us follow God.

The apostle Paul tells us, "The fruit of the Spirit is love, joy, peace, patience, kindness, goodness, faithfulness, gentleness and self-control" (Gal. 5:22-23). The fruit of something is the natural byproduct of that something. For instance, the fruit of an apple tree is an apple. The fruit of an orange tree is an orange. An apple tree doesn't have to cross its fingers and hope for the ability to produce apples. Nor does an orange tree have to discipline itself enough to produce oranges. No, an apple tree produces apples, and an orange tree produces oranges, because their fruit is the outward expression of their inward nature. In the same way, the fruit—the natural byproduct—of living in step with God's Spirit is the fruit of God's Spirit—love, joy, peace, patience, kindness, goodness, gentleness and self-control.

When you become a Christian and understand that God's Holy Spirit has taken up residence in your life, giving you a brand-new nature, the natural outcome is a life that manifests this fruit. No longer do you have to wish for these qualities, nor do you have to perform some religious act of penance to produce these qualities. You need only to yield yourself to God's Spirit and allow the Spirit to produce these qualities in you.

Certainly, habits like prayer, Bible study and attending church help you grow in your relationship with God, but these habits are simply a means to an end—not the end themselves. These habits cultivate your soul in the same way a farmer cultivates his apple trees. A farmer cultivates his trees because he wants the tree to produce fruit. You cultivate your spiritual life because you, too, want fruit—the fruit of the Spirit. The Holy Spirit produces God's nature in you.

When we moved into our home, we planted several fruit trees in our backyard. In my mind's eye, I pictured an abundance of apples, oranges, plums and peaches. I was so disappointed the first year. Each of our trees only produced four or five pieces of fruit, total. Talk about a shock! I envisioned fresh fruit for breakfast and fresh pies for dessert. Little did I know then that sometimes a tree takes years to produce an abundance of fruit. Though the trees did produce some fruit early on, time and cultivation increased the crop. In the same way, a real Christian produces real spiritual fruit. But time spent learning to cultivate dependence on God increases the crop of love, joy, peace, patience, kindness, goodness and faithfulness, gentleness and self-control in a believer's life.

The Christian life can't be lived merely by trying; it has to be lived by trusting. The key, however, is allowing the Spirit the freedom to work in your life. Before any of this can take place, a person must first meet God.

## The Holy Spirit Helps Us Meet God

My sweet friend Brittany became a Christian just six months ago. Brittany, a beautiful 22-year-old college coed, has a past you might never guess from looking at her. She's addicted to alcohol. Nearly three years ago now, Brittany faced her addiction head-on and joined a 12-step program. It wasn't a pretty journey. Nor was it easy. In fact, her road to recovery was littered with lies and lapses. But on her road to recovery, Brittany began considering—for the first time ever—the possibility that God might exist. The "higher power" that the 12-step program refers to in its meetings seemed to make sense to Brittany, causing a formerly skeptical party girl to join the Bible study I began leading for the spiritually curious.

As we began exploring God's Word, Brittany asked insightful questions, leading to some lively discussions. One day, she met her boyfriend for frozen yogurt with a confession: "I can't get God out of my mind. Do you think it's weird that I feel almost . . . I don't know . . . compelled to seek Him?" Her boyfriend did. She didn't.

And neither do I. What Brittany experienced is what Jesus referred to when He spoke the following words about the Holy Spirit: "Jesus answered, 'Very truly I tell you, no one can enter the kingdom of God unless they are born of water and the Spirit. Flesh gives birth to flesh, but the Spirit gives birth to spirit'" (John 3:5-6). We come to God because the Spirit draws us to Himself. We come into a relationship with God by means of the Holy Spirit. We are identified as God's child because of the Holy Spirit.

---

THE CHRISTIAN LIFE CAN'T BE LIVED MERELY BY TRYING; IT HAS TO BE LIVED BY TRUSTING. 

---

## The Holy Spirit Was Given as a Guarantee

The moment a person places her faith in Jesus Christ for the forgiveness of her sins, God places the Holy Spirit into her heart. The presence of God's Spirit in the life of a believer is the deposit that guarantees the security of eternal life. The apostle Paul explains it this way: "Now it is God who makes both us and you stand firm in Christ. He anointed us, set his seal of ownership on us, and put his Spirit in our hearts as a deposit, guaranteeing what is to come" (2 Cor. 1:21-22).

Fourteen years ago, we purchased a brand-new home. Actually, we purchased what would become a brand-new home, since construction had yet to begin. When we purchased our home, the builder required a deposit. Once we signed on the dotted line, the deposit became nonrefundable, but it also served as an assurance that the house under construction would become ours the minute it was complete. Our deposit guaranteed a home.

In the same way, God gives the Holy Spirit as a deposit guaranteeing an eternal home that will someday be ready for each believer. The deposit is nonrefundable—yours to keep—as your personal guarantee of eternal life. You don't have to hope for heaven. You don't have to wonder if you'll "get in." The Holy Spirit is given to those who trust in Christ's payment for their sins as a seal—a deposit—guaranteeing eternal security. Because the Holy Spirit indwells the believer, she doesn't have to second-guess her eternal destiny. She can know.

## The Holy Spirit Gives Assurance

The Holy Spirit also gives the believer assurance that she is God's child. Sometimes it's easy to doubt our security with God. *Am I really a Christian? Sometimes I fail so miserably, how could God still love me?* Our doubts stem from the belief that somehow our acceptance with God is based on what we do for God, rather than what He has done for us. Religion is spelled "D-O," but Christianity is spelled "D-O-N-E." Religion tells us that we can earn God's approval based on our acceptable works, while Christianity tells us that we receive God's approval based on our faith in Christ's acceptable sacrifice. The Holy Spirit was given to quell our doubts about the authenticity of our relationship with God. Paul explains it this way in his letter to the Romans:

> For all who are led by the Spirit of God are children of God. So you have not received a spirit that makes you fearful slaves. Instead, you received God's Spirit, when he adopted you as his own children. Now we call him "Abba [Daddy], Father." For his Spirit joins with our spirit to affirm that we are God's children (Rom. 8:14-16, *NLT*).

In my own journey, when I have doubted the assurance of my relationship with God, or when I've messed up so badly that I wonder how God could possibly still love me, this passage has given me comfort and hope. I've been adopted as a child. An adopted child is a chosen, permanent member of a family. She is not a guest. Not a slave. Not a temporary visitor. The parent/child relationship is enduring and irrevocable. As God's children, the Holy Spirit assures us of our adoption. We can now call God our "Daddy" by means of His Spirit.

The Spirit of God not only draws us to Himself and gives us security in our relationship with Him, but the Holy Spirit also helps us know all that God has in store for us. Paul wrote, "And we have received God's Spirit (not the world's spirit), so we can know the wonderful things God has freely given us" (1 Cor. 2:12, *NLT*). And he prayed this simple but profound prayer for the believers in the city of Ephesus:

> I keep asking that the God of our Lord Jesus Christ, the glorious Father, may give you the Spirit of wisdom and revelation, so that you may know him better (Eph. 1:17).

I am guessing that you are reading this book because you would like to know God better. If that's the case, the Holy Spirit is working in your life right now—both in ways you can see and in ways you can't—to ensure that you have the wisdom, insight and revelation you need to know Him. You may find yourself unexplainably drawn to a Christian friend. That's the Holy Spirit working in your life. You may feel the desire to attend church. That's the Holy Spirit working in your life. You may feel the need to read the Bible or join a Bible study. That's the Holy Spirit working in your life. You may start to pray. That's the Holy Spirit working in your life. You may sense the need to leave one lifestyle behind for another. That's the Holy Spirit working in your life. You may begin to recall pieces of information you've learned about God at seemingly random moments. That's the Holy Spirit working in your life. You may feel the need for forgiveness or hope or unconditional love. That's the Holy Spirit working in your life.

You may have never recognized the Holy Spirit's presence with you (and if you are already a believer, *in* you), but He's there just the same—leading you, guiding you, helping you and directing you. These are just a few of the ways the Holy Spirit is alive and active in the lives of women like you and me and Brittany.

## The Holy Spirit Helps Us Understand and Apply God's Word

The Holy Spirit helps us follow God by reminding us of and leading us to God's Word. In fact, there's an inseparable link between God's Spirit and God's Word. Jesus told His followers that after His death and resurrection, the Spirit would remind them of all that He had taught them (see John 16:13-15). Just today a dear friend told me about an event that happened this week. A minor family crisis sent her into an emotional tailspin. While feeling a bit panicked, a Scripture she had committed to memory years ago popped into her mind. What Bible passage did my sweet friend remember just when she needed it?

> Don't worry about anything; instead, pray about everything. Tell God what you need, and thank him for all he has done. Then you will experience God's peace, which exceeds anything we can understand. His peace will guard your hearts and minds as you live in Christ Jesus (Phil. 4:6-7, *NLT*).

In the midst of her stress and confusion, the Holy Spirit brought to my friend's mind truth that she had previously learned from God's Word. His Word isn't a power-of-positive-thinking mantra that we name, claim and then move on. We are people with real-life issues and real-life emotions. The Holy Spirit may have to remind us of God's truth over and over and over again. In fact, my friend told me she woke up in the middle of the night, again burdened with worry over the issue facing her family. Once more, the Holy Spirit brought God's Word to her mind. You see, believers have an ongoing, dynamic, life-giving relationship with God's Spirit. As our comforter, counselor and guide, He leads us and directs us in our everyday lives, matching our needs with the truth of God's Word.

God gave us His Spirit as our helper, guide, comforter, counselor and encourager. The Holy Spirit also empowers His children to represent Him to others. He enables us to show grace, compassion and love—to live a life that represents God well. He empowers us to speak up for God.

## The Holy Spirit Makes Us Witnesses

The first chapter of the book of Acts explains this more fully: "But you will receive power when the Holy Spirit comes on you; and you will be my witnesses" (Acts 1:8). In a courtroom, a witness testifies about what he or she has seen, heard or knows. When the Holy Spirit fills our life, we become witnesses for Christ. We can tell others what we have seen, heard or what we know about God—however little or much that might be. The power to share our love and knowledge of God comes from God's Spirit. He equips us to share the good news that God loves people and wants a relationship with them. He empowers us to tell others about who God is and how to meet Him personally.

When it comes to sharing your faith in God, it's not only what you know, but more importantly, it's *who* you know. If you know God, you can be a witness for Him. With the help of the Holy Spirit, you can testify about what you have seen, heard and experienced in your journey with Him. You can pass on your faith to those you love.

## The Holy Spirit Prays for Us

My mom wanted to pass on her faith to those she loved—especially her children. She talked openly about her faith in God, but more importantly, she lived it.

I was a grown woman, with children of my own, before my mother revealed her nightly ritual during my growing-up years. Long after my brother, sister and I were tucked in, Mom would make one final check on us before heading to bed herself. While we lay fast asleep, my mom would kneel by each of our beds and pray for us by name. She prayed for our protection, our life direction, our friendships, our future spouses. She prayed for our hopes and our hurts.

This she did night after night, year after year, as we lay sleeping, unaware.

What my mom did for me, the Holy Spirit does for you.

In the same way, the Spirit helps us in our weakness. We do not know what we ought to pray for, but the Spirit himself intercedes for us through wordless groans (Rom. 8:26).

Have you ever felt like you just couldn't pray? Ever felt like you didn't know what to say to God, or even where to start? Has your heart ever been so burdened you simply couldn't choke out the words? Ever been so distraught that your brain couldn't put two sentences together, much less formulate a coherent prayer?

In moments like these, the Holy Spirit is with you. He's kneeling before the Father, praying prayers with groans of compassion and concern so deep they can't even be put into human words. He's bearing your burdens, shouldering your concerns and strengthening you in your weakness.

This He does day after day, year after year, while you lay unaware.

## The Holy Spirit Further Explained

In 1884, Edwin Abbot wrote the novel *Flatland*, an imaginative story about life in a two-dimensional world. The protagonist of the book is A. Square, and, as the name suggests, he's simply a flat shape—just lines on a page. As such, A. Square can only experience a sphere as a flat shape. The concept of depth is simply incomprehensible to him and his fellow Flatlanders.[1]

In many ways, I am A. Square, and so are you. Our human limitations make it difficult to fully envision a divine being. We are three-dimensional characters trying to wrap our minds around four-dimensional concepts. Still, we want to understand God.

I've found that an illustration from science class helps illuminate the mystery. Every grade school age child learns that $H_2O$ manifests itself in one of three ways: a solid, a liquid and a gas. In solid form, $H_2O$ is ice. In its liquid form, $H_2O$ is water, and in its gaseous form, $H_2O$ is steam. Which one is really $H_2O$? The answer, of course, is all three. In the same way, the one God is three eternal persons: Father, Son and Holy Spirit. Which one is God? All three.

God loves you so much that He is committed to your best. Like a tender parent, God encourages you, corrects you, protects you, comforts you, directs you, counsels you and even prays for you in your weakest, most vulnerable moments. He does all this and more by means of the Holy Spirit.

## The Holy Spirit, Our Helper

You can't live the Christian life on your own—at least not the way it was meant to be lived. Fortunately, you don't have to. God's Holy Spirit was given to help women like you and me live the Christian life. He gives us security. He gives us guidance. He reminds us of God's words and leads us into truth. He empowers us to live the Christian life and share this life with others. And He prays for us when we are too weak to pray ourselves.

No, we can't live the Christian life by our own efforts. But what we can't do alone, God does in us, through us and for us, by His Spirit.

## For Further Study

Who is the Holy Spirit? Write down what each of the following verses say about the Holy Spirit:

John 4:24

John 14:16-17

John 14:26

John 16:13

Where was the Holy Spirit "in the beginning," according to Genesis 1:1-2?

Several times throughout the Bible the Holy Spirit is mentioned in conjunction with the Father and the Son. Read the following verses and note how or why the three are mentioned together:

Matthew 28:18-20

Mark 1:9-11

The Holy Spirit is the third person of the Trinity, along with the Father and the Son. It's been said that God the Father initiates salvation, God the Son accomplished salvation and God the Spirit applies salvation.

What do the following verses say about how the Holy Spirit helps us meet God?

John 3:4-6

Ephesians 1:17-18

Titus 3:4-6

According to Ephesians 1:13, when do you receive the Holy Spirit into your life?

A believer receives the gift of the Holy Spirit the moment she places her faith in Christ and comes to know God the Son as her Savior. Because the Holy Spirit indwells all believers, the Holy

Spirit equips us to live the Christian life. God, through His Spirit, works in and through us to help us know Him and follow Him.

Look up the following verses and note how the Holy Spirit helps us in our daily lives:

John 14:26

Romans 5:5

Romans 8:14

Romans 8:16

Romans 8:26-27

Romans 15:13

Galatians 5:13-16

Galatians 5:22-23

Which of the works of the Holy Spirit is most meaningful to you? Why?

The Holy Spirit was never meant to be a mystery. As the third person of the Trinity, He comes alongside to guide us in our relationship with Christ. He helps us, teaches us, comforts us, counsels us, empowers us, convicts us and fills us with God's love.

**Note**
1. R. James, *Thirsty* (Orlando, FL: CruPress, 2008).

# Bible Basics

My father was a division 1 collegiate football coach, so my competitive nature should have come as no surprise to those who knew me as a child. Though I've mellowed into a kinder, gentler version of me, in my younger years I had yet to refine the rough edges that propelled my desire to win.

In second grade, I read a book that, quite frankly, no child with my personality traits should have been allowed to read. Though I can't recall the title, the book was filled with surefire ways to win party games, including one game my friends inevitably played at birthday parties—Pin the Tail on the Donkey. While this handy manual conceded there was no foolproof way to win Pin the Tail on the Donkey apart from cheating, it did, however, outline a little known rule: A secondary prize should always be given to the child whose tail is farthest away from the donkey, in addition to the first place prize awarded to the child whose tail is closest. My eyes widened and my heart beat wildly as my seven-year-old mind unraveled the implications of discovering this life-altering revelation. I would never go home empty-handed from a party again!

Days later, my classmate Debbie had a party. True to form, her mom tacked the vinyl Pin the Tail on the Donkey poster on their family room wall, handed us each a tail and blindfolded the first child. One by one, each of my classmates did their best to pin the tail as close to the donkey as they could, while I stood smugly, arms folded across my chest, confident in my strategy. If only they knew what I knew!

Finally, my turn came. Debbie's mom secured my blindfold, spun me around and set me free. Poor Mrs. Johnson, she actually felt sorry for me when I walked away from the donkey board and headed straight toward the wall on the opposite side of the room. My heart soared with joy when I removed my blindfold and realized no one's tail could possibly be farther away than mine. Mrs. Johnson gave me one of those "Oh, dear, isn't she kind of pitiful?" smiles that grown-ups sometimes give to children they feel sorry for. I'm sure she wondered if I was just a bit on the slow side.

When the last tail had been placed, it was time for prizes. I could hardly wait. Boy, would my friends be surprised when they realized my well-played strategy! Sadly, I was the one left surprised. Mrs. Johnson had a prize for the first place winner. She'd even purchased a prize for the second place child. But there would be no prize for me.

I sat stunned. My smug smile, wiped clean off my face, was replaced with an expression of shock and shame. Hesitantly, I approached Mrs. Johnson and said, "Excuse me, but isn't there supposed to be a prize for the tail farthest from the donkey? I read a book that said there was."

"Oh honey, no. Maybe you misunderstood."

The book had been specific about the last place prize. I was sure of it. I banked my hope on it. I based my entire strategy of game playing on it. I had placed my faith in what I read between the pages of that book.

But the book was wrong.

I trusted a book whose assertions were wrong. My trust in the book determined my actions. I played the game according to my beliefs, but since my beliefs were faulty, my faith proved worthless. Faith is only as good as the object of our faith.

Far too many women play the game of life based on beliefs that in the end fail to deliver, leaving them disillusioned, heartbroken and confused. Here are some common beliefs that fail to deliver:

- *God grades on the curve.*
- *I'll go to heaven because I'm a good person.*
- *It doesn't matter what you believe, as long as you believe in something.*
- *When we die, we die. There's no heaven or hell.*
- *All religions lead to God.*
- *People are nothing more than a set of molecules brought together by time and chance.*
- *The Bible is simply an ancient book with lots of mistakes and errors.*

My faulty, childish belief left no permanent mark, just a brief moment of embarrassment and defeat. But faulty beliefs about God have permanent implications we dare not gamble with. Our faith must be rooted in the truth, backed up by facts and proven over time. For the Christian, the basis of faith rests squarely on God's Word, the Bible. The Bible is the single book that guides our beliefs and practices. The natural question then becomes "Can the Bible be trusted?" If not, the Bible is no more valuable than my second-grade party game book. But if the Bible can be shown to be a reliable source of information about God, then the message of the Bible must be respected and, as we will see, believed and obeyed.

So, why can we trust the Bible? And exactly what is the Bible anyway?

# The Uniqueness of the Bible

Let's start with some basic facts about the Bible. The word "bible" comes from the Greek word *biblios*, which means "book." The Bible is one book, divided into two major divisions—the Old Testament and the New Testament. The Old Testament relays the story of God and His people before the birth of Christ. It begins with creation and outlines the story of the Jewish nation.

The New Testament begins with the life of Jesus Christ and explains the story of God and His people from the birth of Christ on. The Bible is further divided into 66 individual books, written by individual authors—39 Old Testament books and 27 New Testament books. The Bible incorporates different literary genres. Some authors emphasize historical events; some write poetic prayers; others record prophecy; while still others emphasize God's commands and promises. Everything recorded in the Bible, however, has one purpose—to reveal God to people. The overarching theme of the Bible is man's salvation through the promised Messiah, Jesus.

The Bible was written over a period of 1,500 years, on three continents (Asia, Europe and Africa) by more than 40 authors (some wrote more than one book of the Bible) who wrote in three different languages (Hebrew, Greek and Aramaic). These authors came from different cultures—some were Jews and some were Gentiles; some were kings and some were paupers; some were well-educated, and some were not; some were religious leaders, some were political leaders and some were simply ordinary, everyday folks. The variation in the authors' backgrounds is enormous, to put it mildly. With all this disparity, one might expect the Bible to contain different messages, differing perspectives and even differing assertions of truth. But—and here's the mind-blowing part—the Bible has one continuing message from the first book to the last. The likelihood that 40 different people who wrote in three different languages, lived on three different continents and in different eras, would come up with one continual message, one continual theme and one continual plan of salvation is nothing short of miraculous. No other religious book shares the uniqueness of the Bible.[1]

Some people argue, however, that the Bible we have now is not an accurate portrait of what was originally written. They think of playing the telephone game with people who spoke different languages, who lived on different continents for a period of 1,500 years. Obviously, in a game like that, the probability that the message would remain intact would be virtually none. However, critics fail to take into consideration a few key facts. First, Jewish scribes who copied the original Hebrew Scriptures (what we refer to as the Old Testament) considered the words—and even the strokes of the letters—so holy that if they made even one tiny mistake they started transcription over from the beginning, even if the mistake was made at the very end. The ancient scribes left no room for error. They understood the gravity of their task. They copied for their people the very words of God, and therefore tolerated no error or mistake.

In addition, numerous copies of the New Testament parchment and papyrus manuscripts have been found. When scholars compare these early documents to our current rendition of the Bible, they've discovered that what we have now is virtually identical to the original manuscripts. Just how many copies of these ancient manuscripts have been found? 10? 20? 100? Currently, we have 5,795 copies of the Greek New Testament, full or partial manuscripts, and more than 18,000 copies translated into other languages, bringing the total to more than 24,000 copies. To put the enormity of this data into context, the second most available ancient manuscripts are from Homer's *Iliad*, which has 1,757 copies. Scholars have only 251 copies of

Caesar's *Gallic Wars.*[2] Most ancient documents have fewer than 25 copies. In fact, compared with other ancient pieces of literature, the Bible has more manuscript evidence than any 10 pieces of classical literature *combined.*[3]

The fact that so many copies of the New Testament have been found doesn't prove that the Bible is true, but it does prove that it's historically reliable. Because of the enormous number of ancient manuscripts, we can be confident that the Bible we read today is virtually identical to the Bible written nearly 2,000 years ago.

When discussing the reliability of the Bible, it's also important to note the qualifications of the authors and the time between the actual events and the date of writing. Who wrote the Bible? Moses was the author of the first five books of the Old Testament, which Jews call the Torah or Pentateuch. Eyewitnesses of Jesus, or those who interviewed eyewitnesses, wrote the first five books of the New Testament. For instance, Matthew and John were two of Jesus' original 12 disciples, while Mark was the traveling companion of Peter, also one of the original 12. Luke painstakingly interviewed many eyewitnesses, carefully researching before writing his gospel.

Scholars also want to know how much time passed between the actual events and the date of writing. The accounts of Christ's life were written shortly after Jesus' death and resurrection. The overwhelming majority of biblical scholars date the writing of the New Testament between AD 40 and 100, and many believe the entire New Testament was written by AD 80, leaving only a brief gap between the events and their written documentation. Further, there is a mere 40-year gap between the original writing and the earliest copies that have been discovered. At first glance, this gap may seem wide, but it pales when you consider that many of the ancient writings we studied in high school and college, like Homer's *Iliad,* Caesar's *Gallic Wars* or Plato's *Tetralogies,* have gaps as wide as 1,300 years.[4] Scholars don't question the validity of these ancient writings, yet the New Testament has even more historical evidence than many pieces of ancient literature that we readily accept.[5]

The Bible, then, is unique in its historical reliability. No other ancient work is more documented, more researched and more scrutinized than the Bible. The findings confirm the historicity of the Bible. But the Bible also claims to be unique in its origin. What does the Bible say about itself? Does the Bible make any truth claims? Do the actual Scriptures assert any divine origin?

The Bible makes bold declarations about its origin and its power. The apostle Paul wrote these words to his protégé Timothy: "All Scripture is inspired by God" (2 Tim. 3:16, *NLT*). The apostle Peter wrote, "Above all, you must understand that no prophecy of Scripture came about by the prophet's own interpretation of things. For prophecy never had its origin in the human will, but prophets, though human, spoke from God as they were carried along by the Holy Spirit" (2 Pet. 1:20-21). Clearly, these are bold assertions. The Bible declares itself to be the very words of God—God-inspired (God-breathed). If this is true, then you might expect its words to be life transforming.

And they are.

## The Bible Contains Promises to Claim

When I was in college, one of my roommates, Susie, was an avid runner. One day, she changed into her running shoes and shorts, and bounded out the door for what would become a life-altering run. While jogging the streets surrounding UCLA, she happened upon a well-dressed woman lying unconscious on the sidewalk. Susie shouted for help, but no one came. She knelt down, cupped the helpless stranger's face in her hands, and began breathing life into her, silently praying as she worked.

Susie continued as the seconds ticked by, when seemingly out of nowhere, an ambulance arrived. Someone had heard her cries for help and called 911. The paramedics whisked the unconscious woman away, but Susie couldn't get the woman out of her mind. Hours later, she called the hospital. "Are you the young woman who performed CPR until the paramedics arrived?" the voice on the other end of the line asked Susie. "You saved her life."

We read in Psalm 19:7, "The instructions of the LORD are perfect, reviving the soul" (*NLT*). In other words, what Susie did for the helpless woman, God's Word does for us—it revives our souls.

In truth, sometimes I am the helpless woman in need of reviving. Sometimes the day in, day out responsibilities of life, work, home and family leave me depleted. Add an occasional heartache or unforeseen crisis and I'm ready to collapse, even if only metaphorically speaking. I need someone or something outside myself to breathe life into me. I need to be revived, renewed and restored in body, mind and soul. God's Word is just what I need in times like these. God's Word is perfect, reviving the soul.

Six years ago, I went through a season of heartache and pain. Medical issues, work stress and a major life change took its toll on my otherwise upbeat, positive outlook on life. I was beaten down from a series of events that kept crashing down like thundering waves against the shore. Just when I felt like I could come up for air, another wave of heartache would come crashing over me, leaving me treading water. I was growing weary and sinking quick. During this difficult season, my husband ended up in ICU for seven long days. On day five, I received a phone call from my well-meaning brother.

"How are you doing, sis?" he asked.

"Truthfully, not very well," I responded, as tears rolled down my cheeks.

"God has a purpose in all of this, you know," he said in an attempt to encourage.

Did I believe that God had a purpose in my pain? Yes. Did I believe that ultimately God would use our circumstances, as trying as they were, for good? Yes, with all my heart. But what I needed at that moment wasn't a platitude of how God would *eventually* work all the messy, painful circumstances out according to His plan. I needed something in the moment. My soul needed reviving *now*.

I squeezed my eyes shut to hold back the tears, "But, Rog, I am brokenhearted."

Silence followed as the weight of my pain settled into my brother's realization. Finally, he spoke softly and with compassion.

"Oh, sis, God is near to the brokenhearted."

His words were healing balm to my broken soul. They were straight from God's heart to mine. We read in Psalm 34:18, "The LORD is close to the brokenhearted." God's Word—words from the Bible—revived my soul. They were able to penetrate my heart and give me hope in the midst of pain. The writer of Hebrews declares, "The word of God is alive and active" (Heb. 4:12). God's Word is alive, filled with life and, therefore, able to breathe life into a soul in need of reviving—a soul like mine, a soul like yours. My circumstances aren't always perfect, and I'm guessing your circumstances aren't always perfect either, but "The instructions of the Lord are perfect, reviving the soul." God's promises, like this one, transform our lives.

God's Word contains hundreds of life-giving promises like the one that revived my soul that day.

- "I will never leave you nor forsake you" (Josh. 1:5).
- "My grace is sufficient for you, for my power is made perfect in weakness" (2 Cor. 12:9).
- "I can do all things through him who gives me strength" (Phil. 4:13).
- "My God will meet all your needs" (Phil. 4:19).
- "Look at the birds of the air; they do not sow or reap or store away in barns, and yet your heavenly Father feeds them. Are you not much more valuable than they?" (Matt. 6:26).
- "You will seek me and find me when you seek me with all your heart" (Jer. 29:13).
- "The very hairs of your head are numbered" (Matt. 10:30).
- "'I know the plans I have for you,' declares the LORD, 'plans to prosper you and not to harm you, plans to give you hope and a future'" (Jer. 29:11).
- "If any of you lacks wisdom, you should ask God, who gives generously to all without finding fault" (Jas. 1:5).
- "Come to me, all you who are weary and burdened, and I will give you rest" (Matt. 11:28).

These are just a few of the many promises God has made to people who seek Him. They are more than slick clichés or inspirational mantras; these are promises made by God to women like you and me. When we claim them, God's promises have the power to transform our lives.

# The Bible Contains Commands to Obey

God's Word transforms our lives in other ways too. "For the word of God is alive and active. Sharper than any double-edged sword, it penetrates even to dividing soul and spirit, joints and marrow; it judges the thoughts and attitudes of the heart" (Heb. 4:12). God's Word is the plumb line for our attitudes and actions. King David prayed, "Guide my steps by your word, so I will not be overcome by evil" (Ps. 119:133, *NLT*).

The Bible is filled with God's promises, but it is also filled with God's commands. These commands are to help us, to instruct us and guide us in right living. Right living leads to joy. That's why David prayed, "Make me walk along the path of your commands, for that is where my happiness is found" (Ps. 119:35, *NLT*).

God's commands are never random or senseless; neither are they intended to make our lives a drag filled with the drudgery of trying to obey a million meaningless lists of religious dos and don'ts. Rather, God's commands are intended to bless us, protect us and guide us. Put bluntly, God's laws are meant to keep us from doing something stupid, harmful or evil. God's commands and instructions provide real-life wisdom—and who couldn't use a dose of wisdom on a daily basis?

When our daughter Kylie was in fifth grade, she was invited to sleep over for a classmate's tenth birthday party. I arrived the next morning only to be greeted by the birthday girl's father. Apparently, he had something to discuss with me that he wanted to say privately. "Mrs. Jones, may I speak with you about your daughter?" he began. To be candid, I fantasized about telling him no before speeding out of his driveway at about 90 miles an hour. But in real life, what we'd *like* to do isn't always the best option. So, I slapped a polite smile on my face and responded brightly, "Of course!"

He went on to explain that the previous night the girls brought out a DVD to watch—a PG-13-rated DVD. When Kylie saw the rating, she apologized and explained that she wasn't allowed to watch a PG-13 movie without our permission. This, of course, infuriated the other girls. "Come on, Kylie, just watch the movie. You'll ruin the party if you don't," they pleaded. According to her friend's father, Kylie sweetly explained once again why she couldn't watch the movie. So the girls tried another tactic—rationalization. "Kylie, if our parents say it's okay to watch the movie, your parents will say it's okay." When rationalization failed, they moved on to deception. "How will your parents even know you watched the movie? We won't tell, if you don't." But Kylie kindly but firmly held her ground. Finally, the birthday girl's parents (who stood listening to the whole drama in the kitchen) intervened, suggesting a movie everyone could watch and enjoy.

The father ended his recollection of the night's events with these words: "When my wife and I got in bed last night, we looked at each other and said, 'How did this child learn to stand up to such intense peer pressure?' Whatever she's got, we want it for our child."

Needless to say, my heart burst with pride as Kylie belted herself into the backseat of our SUV. "Honey, I heard what you did last night, and I am so proud of you."

"Well, of course I wouldn't watch that movie," she said with a shrug.

"Really? Why not?"

"Mom, I only did what you have been praying for me every night of my life. When you put me to bed, the last thing that you pray is always the same: 'And, dear Lord, please help Kylie to choose to do right, even if everyone else around her chooses wrong.'"

Why had I prayed that prayer? Why had I tried to teach her to choose right over wrong—even in small matters like getting permission before watching a questionable movie? Was it because I want to make her life miserable? A bore? A drag? No, it's because I love her more than life itself, and I want to protect her from harm and empower her to grow up to be a woman with the courage, integrity and guts to do what is right despite popular opinion.

Little girls who make the right choices grow up to be women who make the right choices. These women are free. They're happy. They're strong. They're confident. They're wise. They're on the path of life as it is meant to be lived. I gave my daughter guidelines, not to inhibit her happiness, but to ensure it.

God gives us His instructions for the same purpose. His Word keeps us on the path that brings life; it keeps us from harm, unnecessary heartache and hardship; it keeps us from any evil we might do to ourselves or to others; and it keeps us from the evil others might do to us. God's Word is a light to our path. If we obey it, it has the power to transform our lives.

## The Bible Contains Examples to Follow

God's Word is filled with promises and commands, but the Bible is also filled with stories. These stories—historical narratives—provide insight into how real people walked (or failed to walk) with God. Their stories serve as role models to follow, and sometimes, as examples to avoid. Their accounts teach us about how God deals with people and how events reveal God's larger plan for mankind. They serve as a reminder that every life—yours included—matters to God.

In Christian circles a popular saying goes like this: "Watch how you live . . . your life might be the only Bible a person ever reads." If a picture is worth a thousand words, then a life well lived is worth a thousand sermons. We learn about God not only by what we hear or read; we also learn about God by how we see Him work in the lives of those around us. The Bible is filled with stories of people like you and me whose lives illustrate what it means to know God. They aren't perfect people. Mercifully, the Bible records their failures as well as their successes. They are simply human. Their stories, their histories and their life events reveal God's character, God's plan for history and God's passion for a relationship with people. Their stories shed light on our stories.

## The Bible Contains Truth to Believe

The Bible contains promises to claim, commands to obey, examples to follow and, perhaps most importantly, truth to believe. Jesus said, "You will know the truth, and the truth will set you free" (John 8:32). When we base our lives on falsehood, we're left in bondage. A life based on lies may look appealing, but it is ultimately a dead-end path headed nowhere or at least nowhere good. In contrast, knowing the truth leads to freedom—intellectually, spiritually, emotionally, relationally and eternally.

The night before Jesus' crucifixion, the Roman governor Pilate questioned Jesus:

> "You are a king, then!" said Pilate.
>
> Jesus answered, "You say that I am a king. In fact, the reason I was born and came into the world is to testify to the truth. Everyone on the side of truth listens to me."
>
> "What is truth?" retorted Pilate (John 18:37-39).

Reread Pilate's last statement. His question may be the most important question any person can ask: What *is* truth?

Plain and simple, Jesus said, "[God's] word is truth" (John 17:17).

Repeatedly, Jesus used the phrase "truly, truly, I say to you." In effect, Jesus was saying, "Listen to me. What I'm telling you is true." God's words are reliable. His words are certain. His words contain the path to life. The Bible claims to be the very word of God, filled with grace and truth. It claims to be a source of wisdom and insight for living. In other words, the Bible declares itself a reliable source to find life now and life everlasting. The Bible is filled with God's promises for us to claim, His commands for us to obey and truths for us to believe.

What my second-grade party book failed to deliver, God's Word does. The party book offered me a foolproof game plan for winning. I thought the book was right. I thought the book was true. I thought its message was reliable. But I was wrong, because the book was wrong. The Bible, however, stands alone as singularly unique. It is historically reliable. It is life transformational. It contains the very words of God. The Bible can be trusted, its commands followed, its promises depended on. The Bible is God's message to mankind—every word inspired, every word true.

It's the only reliable source for winning the game of life.

## For Further Study

What does God's Word, the Bible, say about itself?

2 Samuel 22:31

2 Timothy 3:16

1 Thessalonians 2:13

2 Peter 1:20-21

Look again at the verses above, how much Scripture is inspired (God-breathed)?

Why do you think this is important to understand?

According to 1 Timothy 3:16-17, Scripture is helpful in four ways. What are they? Write down the dictionary definition of each.

Many women feel that the Bible is hard to understand. But God has given us an aid to enable us to better comprehend His Word. Based on John 14:26, who is that aid and how does He help us?

Look up 1 Corinthians 2:9-14. Why do we need the Holy Spirit's help to understand God's Word?

Reading God's Word was never meant to be merely an intellectual exercise. God's Word was written to change our lives. But first, we must know His Word. To know God's Word, we must read it or hear it. For many women, reading God's Word can be daunting. Have you ever said or thought any of the following statements? Put a check beside any that apply to you.

- ❏ I can't read the Bible because I don't know where to start.
- ❏ I can't read the Bible because I don't have enough time.
- ❏ I can't read the Bible because I don't know enough about it.
- ❏ I can't read the Bible because I'm not smart enough to understand it.
- ❏ I can't read the Bible because I think I would find it boring.
- ❏ I can't read the Bible because only really religious people do that, and I'm not that religious.

According to the following verses, how does God's Word help us grow in our relationship with God?

Psalm 1:1-3

Psalm 19:7

Psalm 119:9

Psalm 119:11

Psalm 119:28

Psalm 119:66

Psalm 119:105

Psalm 119:143

Psalm 119:165

Hebrews 4:12-13

God's Word provides God's perspective and God's provision
for our needs. Which of the above verses is most meaningful
to you? Why?

How long will God's Word last (see Isaiah 40:8)?

Look up James 1:22-25 and Deuteronomy 29:29. How should we respond to God's Word?

Read Mark 4:1-20. Jesus tells a story about a farmer sowing seeds into four kinds of soil. This is a story that represents a truth about people. What does the seed represent? What does the soil represent, and what are the four kinds of soil Jesus described?

What does each of these four soils represent when applied to the human heart?

To which of the soils can you most relate? Which soil would you most like to represent your life?

**Notes**
  1. Josh McDowell, *The New Evidence that Demands a Verdict* (Nashville, TN: Thomas Nelson, 1999).
  2. D. C. Jones, "The Bibliographical Test Updated," *Christian Research Journal*, 2012.
  3. Josh McDowell, *More Than a Carpenter* (Carol Stream, IL: Tyndale House, 1977).
  4. Jones, "The Bibliographical Test Updated."
  5. Bruce M. Metzger and Bart D. Ehrman, *The Text of the New Testament; Its Transmission, Corruption, and Restoration* (New York: Oxford University Press, 2005).

# 6

# Faith Is Not a Feeling

Dr. Martin Luther King, Jr. said, "Faith is taking the first step even when you don't see the whole staircase." Personally, I think having faith can be difficult. In all candor, I even had trouble finding enough faith to marry my husband (and they say men have commitment issues!).

JP and I dated five years before we married. Our first three years together unfolded in near perfect bliss. I can even recall feeling sorry for other couples who, I naively thought, could never possess the bond we shared.

I was such an idiot.

As the third year of our relationship came to a close, things got rocky. College graduation loomed, and with it, plans for the future. Our dating relationship was suddenly thrust into new territory—the possibility of permanence. Can I be brutally honest? I was scared. Mostly, I worried that JP wouldn't be able to provide for me the way I had hoped a husband would provide. At the time, he worked for a mission organization that paid very, very little. I, on the other hand, had just earned a degree from a prestigious university and was well on my way to financial freedom and success. I loved JP, but a lifetime commitment? I just wasn't sure.

Looking back, I realize I was filled with pride, doubt and fear—some of it warranted, some not. Essentially, I wanted my decision to take the plunge into matrimony to come with a guarantee. My lack of faith in him eventually took its toll and we broke up.

I was miserable without him. He was miserable without me. We got back together, but broke up once again. We were on again then off again, and the cycle would repeat. My doubts and fears and my pride left us tossed on a sea of indecision that lasted nearly two more years. Looking back, it's a miracle he kept pursuing me.

During our last breakup, I began seeing other people, even meeting one young man's extended family. I had no idea that while I was busy meeting my new beau's Grandma, Grandpa, aunts and uncles, JP sat in my parents' living room asking my father for permission to marry me. Of course, Dad was a bit confused over the whole situation. *Why was one young man here, in our home, when I was out with another?* he wondered. It wasn't exactly the dream scene every girl envisions when she gets engaged.

Since JP had no idea about the "other man" (who, as chance would have it, was in graduate school with JP), he expected my father to open his arms wide, welcome him into the family and eagerly grant him permission to ask for my hand in marriage. Instead, JP got a two-hour lecture on the importance of commitment in marriage. Undaunted (and still unaware of the other young man), JP asked me to marry him two days later.

I asked for a week to think it over.

One year later, we still were not engaged, although now we were dating exclusively (I told you it was a miracle he kept pursuing me). At the time, JP was in graduate school, enrolled in a course taught by one of the nation's most respected marital and premarital counselors. One afternoon, the professor lectured on what to do when counseling a couple who has dated for a long period of time but who can't commit. JP leaned forward in his chair and began taking copious notes. Whatever the professor said to do, we were going to do.

The professor recommended working through a workbook designed specifically to help answer questions and concerns of couples contemplating engagement. He also suggested setting a date where the couple would agree to either get engaged or break off the relationship permanently. JP bought the workbook and set the date (February 1), and the clock began to tick. We worked through our individual workbooks separately, and then shared our answers on issues like finances, expectations, role responsibilities, children and religion. The more we talked in concrete terms about each other's hopes, dreams and expectations, the more my worries and doubts faded away. Information became confirmation. With the doubts that plagued my mind erased, my fear and pride melted, and my heart was set free to commit.

But make no mistake; getting married is an act of faith. Twenty-five years later, I realize my decision to marry JP was the second best decision I've ever made (keep reading for the first!).

As I said, I think having faith can be difficult sometimes. And not just in matters like marriage, but also in questions about God.

Does my confession surprise you? It really shouldn't. Plenty of people in the Bible struggled with faith too. Let's face it, it's hard to believe when we can't see, touch, taste or hear something, isn't it? We want evidence. We want proof.

Before I became a Christian, I would often look at people of faith and wonder, *How can they be so sure? How can anyone really know if God is real?* I had a boatload of questions, and when someone dismissed those questions, patted my hand and smiled benignly, telling me to "just believe," I hated it. If God was real, I wanted to know Him. If not, well then, I felt like we should all just call it a day and go home.

And then there were the issues of doubt, fear and pride that made finding faith tricky—the very same issues that thwarted my faith in JP and kept me from taking the step of commitment to marriage.

Still, something in me drew me toward the idea of God. But faith didn't come easy. I like what is concrete. I like the sure bet. I like proof. Maybe you can relate.

One of Jesus' original 12 disciples was just like me.

His name was Thomas. Perhaps you've heard of him; if not, you're going to love this guy. Sometimes he's referred to as "doubting Thomas," although as we will see, Jesus never called him that. His story picks up after Jesus' death and resurrection:

> Now Thomas (also known as Didymus), one of the twelve, was not with the disciples when Jesus came. So the other disciples told him, "We have seen the Lord!" But he said to them, "Unless I see the nail marks in his hands and put my finger where the nails were, and put my hand into his side, I will not believe" (John 20:24-25).

What precipitated Thomas's remarks? The other disciples witnessed the resurrected Christ, in person. Obviously excited, they ran to tell Thomas. Thomas, however, wasn't so quick to believe. He wanted evidence. I can't say that I blame him. In essence, his colleagues asked Thomas to believe in a resurrection based on their testimony alone. Though these men were his closest friends, and no doubt he respected them, Thomas remained skeptical. He had his own set of criteria for belief: He needed proof, and not just any proof, mind you; he wanted to see the nail marks in Jesus' hands and put his fingers in His pierced side. Wow! That's no small order.

Notice what happens next, paying special attention to what Jesus says to Thomas and what Jesus invites him to do:

> A week later his disciples were in the house again, and Thomas was with them. Although the doors were locked, Jesus came and stood among them and said, "Peace be with you!" Then he said to Thomas, "Put your finger here; see my hands. Reach out your hand and put it into my side. Stop doubting and believe" (John 20:26-27).

Jesus didn't berate Thomas for wanting proof. Nor did Jesus scold him by pointing a bony finger in his face as He lectured on the shameful act of doubt, as some might expect. Instead, Jesus met Thomas at his point of concern. Jesus gave Thomas the proof he needed in order to truly believe. He invited Thomas to put his fingers into His side and examine His nail-scarred hands. People who need evidence don't threaten Jesus. Truth doesn't run in the face of scrutiny. It doesn't have to.

Notice Jesus' words to Thomas: "Peace be with you." Peace, the illusive quality that all human beings seek, is the very thing Jesus offered. When our doubts and fears run rampant, peace eludes us. Only when we come to the point of belief can our souls truly experience rest. Jesus could offer Thomas peace of mind, peace of heart and peace of soul, because Jesus *is* peace. Wherever Jesus is, peace is present. It follows then, if Jesus resides in a woman's heart, that her heart rests in peace.

In the months preceding my decision to give my life fully to Christ, I slept restlessly. I could go all day long and never think once about God; but the minute I'd turn out the lights, and all was still, my thoughts turned toward my questions about Christ. Sometimes my doubt-filled mind and heart felt as heavy as the darkness of my room. Alone with my thoughts,

I wrestled with God. *Was He real? How could I know for sure? Would He show me? Would I ever get to the place of true faith?* Interestingly, the moment I placed my faith in Christ, on a brisk fall afternoon, I noticed one instantaneous change in my life—peace. Of course, other changes came too, eventually. But peace came immediately.

Peace came immediately to Thomas, as well. Note his response to the evidence Jesus offered. Did he ask for more proof? Did he still refuse to believe? Check it out:

> Thomas said to him, "My Lord and my God!" (John 20:28).

The proof Jesus presented drove Thomas to his knees. Jesus could have demanded faith without offering evidence. God would certainly be within His rights to do so. But in tenderness and mercy, Jesus provided Thomas the proof he needed. Why? Thomas's questions were genuine. Some people question God with callous, prideful demands, rather than from a place of sincerely seeking God. The person who refuses to believe in God, no matter how much evidence he or she is given, ought not to expect anything from God. God isn't in the business of doing dog and pony shows just to impress a person who has no interest in following Him. Thomas's response to God's revelation revealed his heart. Thomas was a sincere seeker who happened to have genuine doubts.

God promises, "The LORD looks down from heaven on the sons of men to see if there are any who understand, any who seek God" (Ps. 14:2). Since Thomas was sincerely seeking the truth, God revealed it. Just as God proved faithful to His promise to Thomas, He'll prove faithful to His promise to you. If you're a woman sincerely seeking God, you'll find Him. If you're a woman who wants to believe but hesitates because of doubt, God can reach you. He can teach you. He can show you the way. In fact, Jesus even expressed a special blessing for those of us who don't have the benefit of living during the time of Christ and, therefore, can't witness the physical evidence, as Thomas did: "Blessed are those who have not seen and yet have believed" (John 20:29).

Clearly, faith involves an unseen element. If you can see, touch, hear, smell or taste something, you don't need to have faith that it exists. The Bible affirms this: "We live by faith, not by sight" (2 Cor. 5:7). The writer of Hebrews tells us that "faith is confidence in what we hope for and assurance about what we do not see" (Heb. 11:1). Faith means believing beyond the optical nerve. Maybe that's why some people claim that faith is simply not for them. What these skeptics fail to understand, however, is that everyone lives by faith in something. *Everyone.* Whether one's faith is in God, karma or a belief of one's own making, we all live by faith. In fact, we live by faith every day.

Every time we step on a plane, we exercise faith that the engineering behind the aeronautical design will supersede gravity. Every time we send our child off to school, we exercise faith that others will take care of her. Every time we follow our doctor's advice, we exercise faith that his or her recommendation will make us well. We have faith in our pilot, our child's teacher and our doctor because we trust them. Just as it is in the physical realm, so it is in the spiritual. As we learn to trust God, we learn what it means to have faith.

Yet, it's this unseen element that makes faith difficult for some. God knows this. Perhaps that explains Jesus' readiness to show Thomas His nail-scarred hands. No doubt, it is part of the reason God became flesh and lived among us. In Jesus, man could see, touch and hear God. It's why God has revealed Himself in creation. Stand at the base of a mountain, on the shore of the ocean or look up at the galaxies above us and you will be hard-pressed to believe our lives are more than just a blip on the radar screen of eternity. Look closely at a pregnant mother, a newborn baby, a budding flower or furry kitten and notice how the intricacies in their designs reveal a master artist. Watch the seasons change or your body age or the morning dawn and you'll see the hand of God. Creation's design points us to its Designer.

God provides every person evidence for faith in Him. God will give you the evidence you need to believe, if you sincerely seek. And because meeting God means beginning a relationship with Him, the process of trusting God works much like the process of learning to trust a human being. The more information you gain about God, the more you will trust Him.

Paul gives us the method for building our faith: "Faith comes from hearing the message, and the message is heard through the word about Christ" (Rom. 10:17). If you want your faith to grow, saturate your mind with God's Word. The Bible is like the workbook JP and I worked through before making our decision to marry. The workbook guided us to find the truth about each other's character, heart and plans for the future. God's Word reveals the same about God. The Bible clarifies God's character, God's heart and God's plan for the future. God's Word helps you to know God; the more you see God for who He really is, the more your faith will be strengthened, your questions answered and your doubts relieved. Faith isn't a blind leap in spite of the facts; faith is a leap based upon the facts.

## Why Is Faith So Important?

Faith is the central ingredient in meeting God. We become friends with God by faith, and we deepen our friendship with

God by faith. Faith is the beginning, the middle and the end of the Christian life. We never outgrow our need for faith. Without faith, it's impossible to please God (see Heb. 11:6). Because faith is essential to meeting and knowing God, it's vital that we understand what it is and what it isn't. Faith is more than mere intellectual assent to the existence of God. Plenty of people believe in a divine being but don't live by faith. Millions of people say they believe in God, but they live life like they don't. Some people even go so far as to espouse the philosophy that it doesn't really matter what you believe as long as you believe in something. But is this real faith?

Faith is belief in God that results in trust in God; and faith is trust in God that results in belief in God. Belief and trust are like two sides of the coin of faith. True faith stands on two key elements: (1) believing that God exists, and (2) believing that He rewards those who seek Him (see Heb. 11:6). Belief and trust go hand in hand. Because faith involves trust, true faith is never passive. Faith is belief that what God says is true, and living like it.

Faith is belief with feet.

Let's suppose that you and I meet at a local café for coffee. When you arrive, I'm already there, seated and sipping a steaming latte. I motion to the chair across from me and invite you to sit, informing you that the café owners have just purchased these chairs. I go on to tell you that the new chairs are not only comfortable and attractive, but they're sturdy too. In fact, they've even been scientifically proven to safely hold up to 500 pounds. Still, you hesitate. The last time you had coffee at this particular café, your chair broke. Obviously, you're gun-shy.

"What's wrong?" I ask. "Don't you have faith that the chair will hold you safely?"

"Oh, yes," you insist.

But do you really believe? Do your actions validate your claim to have faith in the reliability of the chair, or do your actions prove otherwise?

Belief *claims* to trust. Faith sits in the chair.

Faith is belief in action. Faith is trusting God with your life, not just with your words. Faith believes that what God says is true and acts on it. Belief says, "I believe in God." Faith says, "I trust God." Belief says, "I believe in the power of prayer." Faith says, "I pray." Belief says, "I believe in God's word." Faith says, "I obey God's word." Belief says, "I believe God's plans are best." Faith says, "I will trust God's plans are best, even when His plans don't make sense right now." Belief says, "I believe God loves me." Faith says, "I live like God loves me."

Faith sits in the chair; belief just talks about it.

Belief dreams about the wedding. Faith puts a ring on the finger.

## How Do I Get Faith?

How does a woman who has lived her whole life without God start to believe—or perhaps more accurately, start to have faith? And what about the woman who believes in God, but who longs for a deeper connection with Him? How does either woman go from point *A* to point *B* in her faith relationship with God?

It all begins with change—a change of the mind, of the heart and of the will: A person who has questions gets answers; a person whose heart runs cold to the things of God softens; a person who lives only to gratify self recognizes her emptiness. Change is usually precipitated by an event, an experience or an insight. As John Maxwell so aptly puts it, "People change when they learn enough that they're able to, are motivated enough that they want to, or hurt enough that they have to." Faith develops when our intellect is satisfied. Faith buds when our heart is open. And, sometimes, faith springs forth when our life is broken. Our core faith issue is either a matter of the mind, the heart or the will—or a combination of all three.

As I've already mentioned, faith comes as we learn more about God through reading His Word, the Bible. God's Word provides answers to our questions and makes sense of the brokenness we see in the world. But there's a second avenue for increasing our faith: We ask for it.

BELIEF DREAMS ABOUT THE WEDDING.
FAITH PUTS A RING ON THE FINGER.

One of my favorite accounts in the Bible concerns a man who acknowledged the limitations of his faith. His son was sick, having experienced convulsions that threatened his life. In desperation the boy's father sought out Jesus, hoping He could help, though not really sure. The father pleaded with Jesus, "If you can do anything, take pity on us and help us!"

"If you can?" says Jesus. "Everything is possible for one who believes."

Immediately the boy's father exclaims, "I do believe; help me overcome my unbelief!" (Mark 9:22-24).

Now there's an honest response! "I do believe; help me overcome my unbelief!" In essence, the man confessed, "I do have faith, but not yet as much as I need," then boldly continues, "So, Jesus, increase my faith. Help me overcome the stumbling blocks that prevent me from possessing authentic faith." God never ignores a heartfelt cry to help us overcome our unbelief.

How much faith do we need? According to Jesus, just a small amount will do to start. In fact, Jesus told His disciples that if they had faith "as small as a mustard seed" (Matt. 17:20), they could do miracles. This analogy proves poignant when you understand that a mustard seed is the smallest seed known. The key is not worrying about how much faith you *don't* have, but rather, living in light of the faith you *do* have. Faith, like a muscle, grows when it is exercised.

## Barriers to Belief

In much the same way I struggled with my decision to marry JP, we sometimes struggle in our journey of faith. What causes these struggles? The same three factors that reared their ugly heads in my days of indecision to marry my husband: pride, fear and doubt.

Pride says, "Religion is the opiate of the masses." Pride says, "I don't believe, and I won't believe." Pride says, "I am my own God." Pride says, "I worship on the altar of ego and self-gratification." The bottom line is this: If faith involves action, then to profess faith means life change. Frankly, some people aren't ready.

Sometimes pride disguises itself in what looks like legitimate questions but are really a smoke screen for an unwillingness to bow the knee to the Creator. Because my husband is a pastor, he often gets asked about spiritual matters. Sometimes a skeptic will challenge JP with one of the "toughies," hoping to stump him. JP learned long ago to discern a person's real barrier to belief. Before answering a skeptic's question, JP often responds by saying, "That's a great question. But before I answer it, let me ask you a question: If I answer your question to your intellectual satisfaction, will you give your life to Christ?" Almost always the person responds in the negative.

Many times the real barrier to faith isn't a question. The real obstacle to faith is something else. Pride is a very real barrier for millions of people.

*Could pride possibly be your faith barrier?*

Some women deal less with pride but find that fear stifles their faith. If you could get inside the head of a woman who struggles with fear, you would often hear the words "What if?" *What if God isn't real? What if I trust God and He hurts me? What if I believe in God and He doesn't come through like I thought He would? What if other Christians don't accept me? What if I become a Christian and I still have questions?* "What if?" paralyzes a person into inaction. Just as my "what ifs" stunted my ability to commit to marriage, spiritual "what ifs" stunt a person's ability to commit to Christ.

*Could fear possibly be your faith barrier?*

Finally, some women deal not so much with pride or fear as with doubt. The woman who battles doubt wonders, *Can anyone really know for sure?* She has legitimate questions that deserve thoughtful answers, but in the process, she gets stuck in the mire of her own limited humanity while she tries to wrap her mind around a limitless God.

*Could doubt be your faith barrier?*

Whatever your barrier to faith, know this: Your questions, concerns, desires and motives are not unique. God has seen it all. Thankfully, God specializes in dealing with prideful, fearful, doubtful people. How does He respond to people who sometimes struggle to have faith?

He understands them.

He loves them.

He pursues them.

More than 25 years ago, my husband's patience won out. When others would have given up the pursuit, JP didn't. Finding enough faith to commit myself in marriage didn't come easy. But it did come. As I began to understand JP's faithfulness, his character and his love for me, my pride, fear and doubts melted, leaving space for faith to flourish—enough faith that I entrusted my life into his care. It was the second best decision I ever made. Only one decision supersedes it.

More than 35 years ago, I began to understand God's faithfulness, character and love toward me. As I did, my pride, fear and doubts melted, leaving space for faith to flourish—enough faith to entrust my life into His care.

It was the best decision I ever made.

It will be the best decision you'll ever make too.

## For Further Study

Plenty of people in the Bible had doubts and questions about faith. Read John 20:24-29 and answer the following questions:

Which disciple needed proof in order to believe in Christ's resurrection?

What proof did he say he needed?

One week later, he received the proof he needed. What was it?

What was Thomas's response to the evidence?

Jesus says a group of people receive special blessing for their faith. Who are they?

When discussing faith, it's important to define our terms. What exactly is faith? Sometimes it's helpful to know what something is not in order to better understand what something is. Contrary to popular opinion, faith is not a blind leap; nor is faith a feeling. The Bible reveals a working definition of faith. According to Hebrews 11:1, what is faith? What do you think this means?

According to Hebrews 11:6, why is faith important? What two things must we believe in order to have faith?

Where does faith originate (see Heb. 12:2)?

Hebrews 12:2 also refers to the fact that faith is a process. According to the following verses, how does our faith grow?

Romans 1:11-12

Romans 10:17

Our faith also grows when we see the faithfulness of God in our lives. What do the following verses teach about God's faithfulness?

Psalm 100:5

Psalm 108:3-5

Lamentations 3:22-24

Consider your life. Although you may have never been aware of it, God has always been with you. How has God been faithful to you? Can you see evidence of God in your life, even before you had faith in Him? If so, how?

Biblical faith is always coupled with action. When a person truly believes, her actions reflect her belief. Read the following verses and note how each person's faith is expressed in action:

Matthew 9:20-22

Mark 2:1-5

Luke 7:1-10

Which of the above stories resonates the most with you? Why?

James 2:14-19 expands on the concept of faith and action. What is the relationship between faith and deeds?

In order to have true faith, we must believe that God exists and that He rewards those who seek Him (see Heb. 11:6). What are the rewards of faith, according to the following verses?

Acts 15:9

Romans 3:28

Romans 5:1

Ephesians 2:8-9

Ephesians 3:12

1 Peter 1:8-9

What does Galatians 2:20 say about living by faith?

# 7

# Why Are There Jerks in the World, and Am I One of Them?

Let me tell you about the best $254 I ever spent.

At the time, I had two small children and a colicky newborn. I spent most of my days in a foggy haze, trying to navigate life with too few hours of sleep and too many hours trying to pacify a constantly crying baby. One morning, I opened our nearly barren pantry to find only a half-eaten box of Cheerios, the end pieces of sandwich bread, a quarter of a jar of peanut butter and a few cans of veggies. I could delay the inevitable no more. Despite the inconvenience of shopping with three kids in tow, a trip to the grocery store had become a necessity. As I stood with the pantry door open wide, trying to figure out breakfast for my little brood, my mind began recording a mental shopping list. I realized that as long as I was out and about, I could also take care of the paycheck issue. My husband's paycheck had been sitting on our kitchen island for days, and I had yet to find time to make the deposit. Today I would make time.

I packed the kids in the car and headed for the grocery store. All in all, it proved to be a rather uneventful excursion, which, as any mother of small children knows, ranks just under winning the lottery in terms of satisfaction value. With the groceries loaded in our trunk, we made one last stop at the bank. I steered the car through the drive-through ATM, ready to make the long overdue deposit, only to discover the drive-through window had run out of envelopes. I sighed. Why couldn't things be simple? Determined not to lug three kids out of the car for a two-minute errand, I came up with a plan: I would park the car, grab an envelope from inside the bank (right inside the front door) and drive through the ATM once again to make the deposit.

I maneuvered my car slowly through the parking lot, looking right and left as I searched for a spot near the front door. Not a single parking space was vacant. Undaunted, I circled the parking lot again; this time I was willing to park anywhere within earshot of the bank's front door. Still no luck. I inched around the lot a third time, figuring someone would leave soon. But they didn't. Now Ashton began to cry, and I knew from experience that my window of opportunity was about to slam shut if I didn't get the deposit done *now*.

I circled the lot one last time. This time I spied a parking spot right by the front door. There was just one teensy problem—it was a handicapped spot. I hesitated for a brief moment, considering my options. Under normal circumstances the idea of parking in a zone reserved for people with a physical disability would never have entered my mind. But this was no normal circumstance. I needed to make the deposit, and Ashton's whimpers threatened to escalate into wails. Besides, I would only be parked for a minute, two minutes tops. I just needed to grab and go.

I eased into the spot, jumped out of the car, bounded up the steps to the bank, grabbed an envelope and raced back to my car. The whole event took less than 60 seconds. Mission accomplished.

My smile vanished when I turned to see a policeman waiting by my car, arms folded, with a look of disgust across his face. I closed my eyes, took a deep breath and launched into my explanation of what preceded my parking in this spot. My panic spilled forth in words that tumbled over one another as they gushed forth. Yes, I had parked in the handicapped spot, but only for 60 seconds. Did he see the crying infant in the backseat? Surely he could understand my desperation. After all, I'd circled the parking lot three times. Maybe he could find it in his heart to let me off with a warning. I had never done this before and would certainly never do it again.

He stared at me blankly, pulled out a pen and began writing the ticket. Now Ashton was screaming, I was sweating and the policeman was lecturing.

And I just couldn't take it anymore.

I jerked the ticket out of his hand and got back in my car, slamming the door shut for emphasis. Blinking back tears, I watched his motorcycle drive away. Ashton was already bawling enough for both of us, so instead of crying, I squeezed my eyes shut, took a deep breath and screamed. Not profanities. Not words. I just screamed. One of those bloodcurdling, bone-chilling screams you hear at horror flicks. I was in the middle of my own silly nightmare.

My two older children were horrified. They had never seen Mommy behave like this.

"Are you okay, Mom? What just happened?" my six-year-old asked, his eyes as big as saucers.

"Yes, honey. I am fine. It's just that that very, very, *very* bad policeman gave Mommy a ticket she didn't deserve."

"Oh." Silence.

"That was a very, very bad policeman, wasn't he, Mommy?"

Then it hit me. What was I doing? Teaching my children that policemen are *bad*? What kind of example was I providing their pliable little souls? After all, I was the one who broke the law; the police officer was simply enforcing it. Sure, from my perspective, it was a minor infraction, but the minor incident revealed some major character flaws—in me.

The truth is, I don't like to be confronted about my wrong-doings. I'm prone to rationalize breaking the rules. I can justify bad behavior with perfectly logical (but faulty) reasoning. I would rather blame someone else than take personal responsibility for my poor choices. I can flip out if pushed beyond my limits. I'm sometimes a bad role model for my children. And the list could go on.

That $254 ticket bought me something more valuable than a fabulous pair of shoes or a fancy trinket for my home. It bought me insight into my soul. It turned the spotlight on the dark places in my heart and revealed ugliness I can normally keep concealed. It exposed a truth I couldn't deny.

I am flawed.

And so are you.

It's what the Bible calls sin, and it affects every single one of us.

Was that parking infringement the biggest sin I've ever committed? Not even close. In fact, looking back, the whole scenario makes me laugh. Given the circumstances, I understand why I responded the way I did. In the grand scheme of life, that little incident is a minor blip. But sometimes the small things reveal larger issues going on underneath. My behavior that day—however justifiable it seemed—opened my eyes to the reality of a character gap in my life. A gap I never even knew existed, or at least never took the time to contemplate.

These gaps lie deep inside every one of us.

## What Is Sin, Anyway?

Technically speaking, the word "sin" means "to miss the mark." In biblical times, "sin" was an archery term. When an archer shot an arrow, the distance between the bull's-eye and where the arrow landed was called "sin." Sin was any distance—great or small—between the arrow and the intended target. Sin is missing the mark of perfection. No wonder the phrase "nobody's perfect" is universally understood to be true. It *is* true.

Generally, most people think of sin as one of the "biggies." Stuff like murder, theft, armed robbery, adultery. Maybe some "minor" infractions like lying might be included in our list of "sin." Hardly any of us would view my behavior on the day I received my ticket as sin (although it was). But when we think of sin as only obvious wrongdoing—the stuff criminals go to jail for, or jerks alienate others by—we miss the real meaning, and the real impact. Sin is missing the mark of perfection. Sin is anything we say, think or do that stands in opposition to God's perfect righteousness, goodness, holiness or love. Therefore, all of us are sinners.

The Bible paints a bleak picture of sin's poison. Sin separates us from God. It separates us from one another. It enslaves us in bondage. It causes fights and quarrels and factions and dissensions. It leads to hopelessness, helplessness and spiritual death. Sin causes hurt and anger and jealousy and revenge. Sin leads us down paths we have no business following. Sin breaks people's hearts and binds people's souls.

Maybe you can relate to these consequences. If you've ever experienced a broken relationship; ever been betrayed by someone you trusted; ever been lied to or lied about; ever been the victim of someone else's (or your own) anger; ever chosen a path that led to heartache or emotional, physical or spiritual destruction, then you've experienced the effects of sin.

When sin entered the world, life was forever changed. God gave the first man and woman, Adam and Eve, one simple command. They could eat anything they wanted from the Garden of Eden—anything at all—except the fruit from one tree. Sounds easy enough, doesn't it? But filled with doubts about God's word and God's goodness, Eve believed Satan's lie. "Did God *really* say . . . ?" began Satan's ploy. Eve took the bait, questioned God's command and did the one thing God told her not to do. Temptation won out. The result? Adam and Eve, who had previously enjoyed unobstructed oneness with each other and with God, felt the first pangs of shame and hurled the first jabs of blame.

The human race has been playing the shame and blame game ever since. Don't believe me? The next time you witness (or participate in) a conflict at home, at the office or at school, notice how often words meant to shame or blame get tossed about. Then notice how the shame/blame game affects the relationships involved. Sin. Shame. Blame. The cycle repeats itself in a million different lives in a million different ways every day. In fact, the day I got my $254 ticket, I became trapped in its cycle. I broke the law. I felt ashamed of my actions. But rather than taking responsibility for them, I blamed the police officer. Sin, shame, blame. Make no mistake; sin affects the actions of real people like you and me.

A life filled with sin is nobody's picture of a party—at least not over the long haul. Sure, sin has its allure. Sin can seem like no big deal. It can even look attractive. If it didn't, no one would ever fall prey to its insidious grip. Satan tempted Eve by holding out the supposed "benefits" of disobeying God. Doing her own thing, rather than God's thing, seemed advantageous. It looked appealing. It looked fun. It looked harmless. It even looked like the smart choice. Sadly, it wasn't. Anyone who has ever been held in the clutch of sin or knows someone who has can attest to the destructive power it can hold over the human life.

In one of her last interviews on *Oprah*, Oprah Winfrey interviewed J. K. Rowling, author of the *Harry Potter* series. Rowling made a fascinating remark during their conversation. She recounted the email she received from her New York-based editor immediately following the terrorist events of 9/11. His last line read, "and they say we shouldn't teach children about evil." There is evil on earth, every bit as much as in any work of fiction we could create.

And it takes its toll on us and on those around us. On those we love. Sin affects us all—those among us who think of ourselves as "good people," and those among us who don't. It's imperative that we grasp that sin resides in us, every bit as much as it resides in "them." If we don't understand our own flawed nature, we won't understand our true need for God.

Jesus had dinner with a man who needed to learn this lesson. His name was Simon, and he was a religious leader back in the day. Simon hears that Jesus is a prophet. Skeptical but curious, he invites Jesus to his home for dinner. While they dine, an "immoral" woman arrives with a perfume-filled jar. She sits at Jesus' feet, anointing His feet with the precious oil (a common practice in biblical times). She's so overcome by Jesus' acceptance of her that she begins to cry. Simon is disgusted.

Their story picks up in Luke 7:39-50:

> When the Pharisee who had invited him saw this, he said to himself, "If this man were a prophet, he would know what kind of woman is touching him. She's a sinner!"
>
> Then Jesus answered his thoughts. "Simon," he said to the Pharisee, "I have something to say to you."
>
> "Go ahead, Teacher," Simon replied.
>
> Then Jesus told him this story: "A man loaned money to two people—500 pieces of silver to one and 50 pieces to the other. But neither of them could repay

him, so he kindly forgave them both, canceling their debts. Who do you suppose loved him more after that?"

Simon answered, "I suppose the one for whom he canceled the larger debt."

"That's right," Jesus said. Then he turned to the woman and said to Simon, "Look at this woman kneeling here. When I entered your home, you didn't offer me water to wash the dust from my feet, but she has washed them with her tears and wiped them with her hair. You didn't greet me with a kiss, but from the time I first came in, she has not stopped kissing my feet. You neglected the courtesy of olive oil to anoint my head, but she has anointed my feet with rare perfume.

"I tell you, her sins—and they are many—have been forgiven, so she has shown me much love. But a person who is forgiven little shows only little love." Then Jesus said to the woman, "Your sins are forgiven."

The men at the table said among themselves, "Who is this man, that he goes around forgiving sins?"

And Jesus said to the woman, "Your faith has saved you; go in peace" (*NLT*).

Simon's problem, of course, was that he separated the "haves" and the "have nots." We still do this today. "Well, I may not be perfect, but I haven't done *that*," we say with our smug judgmental attitude. But in judging others, we judge ourselves. Who among us is perfect?

Others struggle not with self-righteousness, but with self-condemnation. *Because I have done such-and-such, God could never forgive me,* we think to ourselves. And yet, it's not the person who is perfect who's accepted by Christ, but the person who knows she isn't.

It's as simple as this: The woman who thinks she's been forgiven little loves little. The woman who realizes she's been forgiven much loves much.

If we don't understand our need for forgiveness, we will never see our need for God. If we fail to grasp our need for God, we will never love God. We will never have—or even want—a relationship with God. It's only when we confront our own sin problem—no matter how big or how small—that our eyes are opened to the magnitude of God's offer of unconditional love, acceptance and forgiveness.

Jesus came for one primary reason: to reconcile us to God by paying the price for our sins. One of the most powerful verses in the Bible is one you just might skip over if you fail to understand its significance: "The wages of sin is death, but the gift of God is eternal life in Christ Jesus our Lord" (Rom. 6:23). The price tag for sin is death—spiritual and physical separation from God. That's a huge price tag. Who would ever be willing to take on that kind of debt for me? Only one who loved me more than I could imagine

That person is Jesus.

He came to pay the price for my sins and for yours. He came to die in your place, for your sins. Why? Because He loves you that much. Realize this: When you allow Christ to pay your debt by accepting what He did for you on the cross, your debt is paid in full. You are free! You are no longer a slave to sin and its viselike grip around your life.

Let's go back to my parking ticket scenario. Suppose I'm called to appear before a judge to pay my $254 ticket. When my case is called, I stand before the court and am asked how I plead. I answer "guilty," of course. Hearing the verdict, the judge bangs his gavel on the stand and orders me to pay the fine. The harsh sound reverberates in my ears as I dig into my purse, searching for my checkbook. But then the judge does something that stuns the court. Silently, he stands, slips off his judicial robe, walks to my side, takes out his wallet and pulls out $254 in crisp, new bills. My judge pays my fine.

It would be incredible, wouldn't it?

This is exactly what Jesus did for us. We all stand before a holy God, culpable of wrongdoing, owing a debt. In justice, God declared us guilty. In mercy, He took off His royal robe, came down to our side and paid our debt by dying on the cross. The apostle Paul put it this way:

> For it is by grace you have been saved, through faith—and this not from yourselves, it is the gift of God—not by works, so that no one can boast (Eph. 2:8-9).

Incredible, isn't it?

## Is Sin Really a Big Deal?

It can be tempting, however, to think that ignoring our sin is the easiest route to personal peace. *Why deal with the negative stuff? Why not just try to do better next time and move on?*

Some try to sweep their sin under the rug by justifying sinful behavior with rationalization. *It's no big deal. Everyone does it. I only did what I did because he . . . If she hadn't done . . . then I would never have . . .*

Still others dig in their spiritual heels and refuse to admit their sin. *I'm one of the good guys. I try to love my friends and family. I volunteer and give to charity. I don't cheat or lie. Surely I couldn't be classified as a sinner, could I?*

Being a good person can easily blur the image of sin. Let's face it. Some people *are* good people—when compared to other people. But no one is good when compared with God. No one is perfect. *No one.*

My husband likes to recount a story of a man sitting on a plane next to a passenger who began debating the issue of sin. He believed his good works would pave his way to heaven. He was a devoted husband, a good father, a committed employee, a community volunteer. Truthfully, he was an all-around nice guy, someone you'd love to have as your neighbor or co-worker or friend. Given his background, he took issue with the notion of sin. To him, it seemed like out-of-touch religious jargon used to make good people feel guilty about basically nothing. He was convinced that if anyone could make it to heaven by being a good person, his ticket into the pearly gates was a sure thing.

Trying to help the fellow passenger put his life in proper context, the man next to him pulled out a piece of paper and wrote on top, in bold letters, "GOD." Underneath he scribbled a few descriptive words about God—perfectly holy, loving, righteous, good, all-knowing, all-powerful. Stuff like that.

Then he turned to the passenger and asked who, in his opinion, was the most evil person who ever lived. On the bottom of the page he wrote in bold letters the name of that person. He then explained that all people fall somewhere in between the perfection of God and the most evil human among us. Handing his fellow passenger a pen, he asked him to mark where he thought his life would rank. Before he wrote, however, he added one piece of information: Mother Teresa ranked herself only halfway up.

The passenger's eyes softened. "Well, I'm certainly no Mother Teresa," he confessed, as he placed the mark that represented his life and good works well below hers.

The distance between where our life and good deeds rank in comparison to God represents our sin—the distance by how far we fall short of absolute perfection. Are there good people? You bet—when we compare ourselves to one another. Are there sinless people?

Have you ever met any?

# The Solution for Sin

Sin is a real issue for real people.

The burden of guilt, shame and not being good enough is a heavy load to bear. But when we acknowledge our sin to God, rather than finding condemnation, we find forgiveness, mercy and reconciliation. The weight is lifted. We can breathe.

In Christ Jesus, God provided an antidote for the poison of sin. "He was pierced for our transgressions, he was crushed for our iniquities; the punishment that brought us peace was on him, and by his wounds we are healed. We all, like sheep, have gone astray, each of us has turned to our own way; and the LORD has laid on him the iniquity of us all" (Isa. 53:5-6). Jesus' death on the cross satisfied the debt of my sin. Jesus paid the price for me. If I accept His offer of forgiveness, the payment for my sin is paid in full. All I must do is acknowledge my need and receive His gift.

Sometimes, however, acknowledging our need doesn't come easy. No one likes to admit they're "needy." In fact, I've heard people reject Christianity for this very reason. "Christianity is a crutch," they contend. Are they right? Well . . . yes and no. Christianity is not a crutch in the sense that a person has to be down on her luck or put her brain on the shelf in order to believe, as some would argue. But yes, Christianity is a crutch, if by crutch you mean something that enables you to do something you can't do on your own. Sometimes crutches are necessary, and to behave otherwise is, well . . . stupid. If I break my leg and don't use a crutch to help me walk, am I wise or foolish? I'm not a fool for using a crutch if I need one. In fact, admitting my need is the smartest thing I can do.

In the same way, because none of us is perfect, none of us can stand before a perfectly righteous and holy God and gain admittance to His kingdom on our good works. Our good works aren't good enough, if perfection is the standard. We need something that enables us to do what we can't do on our own. We need something—or someone—who bridges the gap between our flawed character and God's perfect one. That person is Jesus. That's why He died on the cross.

Acknowledging our need for God's forgiveness and accepting Christ's free payment for our sin is the bravest, wisest choice a person can make. It takes guts to admit our need. Recognizing my sin and 'fessing up to it is an act of strength, not weakness. Acknowledging a need is the first step toward wholeness in any area of life—emotional, relational, physical or spiritual. In the spiritual arena there's a word for acknowledging our need—"confession."

Confession simply means saying the same thing as God says. In other words, when I agree with God about my behavior by calling my sin, sin, I am confessing. If I say my behavior is "just the way I am" or "a bad habit" or "a personality quirk" or "no big deal," then I am saying something different than God says. I am not confessing. I am justifying. I am excusing. I am denying.

And I am left in bondage.

The Alcoholics Anonymous organization understands the power of confession. That's why its members introduce themselves by stating, "Hi, I'm so-and-so, and I'm an alcoholic." A major component in the success rate found in AA is the reality-check its members experience at each meeting. They don't deny their behavior. They don't justify or rationalize their behavior. They own their behavior. And in doing so, they find freedom and healing. The same principle holds true in the spiritual arena. When we confess our sins to God, we are merely admitting what He already knows. Confession is for our healing, our freedom and our souls.

When I confess and repent of my sin ("repent" means to be headed in one direction when you turn around and head in the other direction—it's doing a 180-degree turn), God is faithful to forgive it. Scripture says, "If we confess our sins, he is faithful and just and will forgive our sins and purify us from all unrighteousness" (1 John 1:9). When I confess my sin to God, He forgives me and—get this—He cleanses me from all unrighteousness. In other words, He wipes my slate clean. Now that's freedom!

Picture a large whiteboard with every sin you have ever committed written in big, black, bold letters for all to see. The words cover everything—all your little white lies, your acts of hatred and jealousy, any sexual immorality you've ever committed. The big, black words written on the whiteboard also include every profanity and every careless, hurtful word you've ever spoken. Now picture Jesus standing before your whiteboard, examining the words that represent your most embarrassing sins. Given what's written there, you might expect to find condemnation and disgust. Instead, Jesus picks up a large eraser and begins wiping the ugly, wretched words away so that no one else has to see what both you and He know. Jesus wipes our slate clean, if we let Him.

When we allow Christ to wipe our sins away, we find the peace our souls long for—peace *with* God and peace *of* God. However, when we ignore, rationalize or refuse to admit our sin, we don't find peace—neither in this life, nor in the life to come. Sooner or later it catches up to us. The only way to find lasting peace is to face our flaws and find forgiveness in Christ.

"There is no one righteous, not even one" (Rom. 3:10). Not me. Not you. Not anyone we know. Every one of us has sinned, which means every one of us is a candidate for a Savior. We all stand guilty before a holy and righteous judge. But God, rich in His mercy, willingly paid the price for our sin.

The best money I ever spent came in the form of a penalty for one ridiculous, stupid sin. The best gift I ever received came in the form of a payment for a lifetime of ridiculous, stupid sins. But my ticket has been paid. And so has yours. It's a gift, if you'll open your life to accept it.

## For Further Study

The word "sin" evokes all kinds of emotions. What connotation does "sin" have for you? Why?

Look up the following verses and note what the Bible says about sin:

Exodus 32:31

Proverbs 14:21

Proverbs 17:19

Acts 8:23

James 2:9

James 4:17

1 John 3:4

1 John 5:17

Were there any actions or attitudes mentioned as sin in the above verses that surprised you? If so, which one(s) and why?

Who or what causes temptation and sin?

Matthew 4:1

James 1:13-15

The word "sin" means to miss the mark. In biblical times, sin was an archery term. When an archer shot an arrow, the distance between the bull's-eye and where the arrow landed was called "sin." Sin was any distance—great or small—between the arrow and the intended target. Sin, then, is missing the mark of perfection.

Read the following verses and note how sin has affected all mankind:

Proverbs 20:9

Romans 3:23

1 John 1:8

What are the consequences of sin?

Isaiah 59:1-3

John 8:34

Romans 6:23

What do the following verses reveal about God's provision for man's sin?

Romans 6:23

Isaiah 53:4-6

Acts 13:38-39

2 Corinthians 5:21

According to the following verses, what are we to do when we realize our sin? With what result?

Psalm 32:1-5

Proverbs 28:13

Luke 5:31

Acts 2:36-39

1 John 1:9

Look over your answers. To whom are we to confess our sins?

For some women, the notion of confession brings back memories of guilt and shame, and perhaps even the feeling of being cornered into admitting something they would rather forget or explain away. Can you relate to any of these feelings? If so, how?

Is there anything in your life that you need to confess right now? Take a moment to write down a prayer of confession below. Then write down 1 John 1:9: "If we confess our sins, he is faithful and just and will forgive us our sins and purify us from all unrighteousness."

Read 1 Corinthians 10:13. What insights do you find regarding how to handle temptation and sin?

# 8

# Talking with God

"I'm on my way to the emergency room and I need you to pray."

"But I don't know how."

"Can you carry on a conversation?"

"Yes."

"Well then, you can pray."

This real-life dialogue took place between two of my friends not long ago. The truth is, most people pray sometime in their life. But it's also true that mystery and confusion surround prayer. Though we generally don't like to admit it, many of us aren't sure we really know how to pray. Is there a "right way" to pray? Are there certain words we should use? Is there a correct way to address God? Is anything too trivial to pray about? Anything too big, or too unimportant? Does God really hear me when I pray? What about moments when I feel like my prayers are bouncing off the ceiling? Why does God say no?

Questions like these swirl around in our heads, never really finding a place to settle until we finally come to understand prayer. Although prayer is widely practiced, it isn't widely understood. Mystery surrounds prayer, even for those who have known God for many years. Fortunately, God's Word provides insight on what, why and how we should pray.

# What Is Prayer, Anyway?

Prayer is simply talking with God. When we read God's Word, the Bible, God talks to us. When we pray, we talk to God. In any relationship, two-way communication is vital. If one person does all the talking (or all the listening), the relationship is skewed.

Prayer isn't talking *at* God. We don't approach God like a spoiled child approaches Santa Claus, demanding everything on our wish list. No, prayer is talking *with* God. Prayer provides a way for us to connect with God; it provides a way for us to bring our needs, cares and concerns before God and find His direction for our lives.

Prayer offers us an opportunity to thank God for His blessings and praise Him for His character. Prayer supplies a way for us to listen to God, to hear Him speak to us through His Word and His Holy Spirit. In healthy, life-giving relationships, communication flows back and forth. Meeting God brings you into a relationship with your Creator. Sometimes He talks to you. Sometimes you talk to Him. That's prayer.

As it is in the human realm, so it is in the spiritual: the better the communication between two people, the better the relationship. When communication flows freely between you and a loved one, you feel a close connection with that person, don't you? You feel understood. You feel encouraged. You feel motivated. You feel loved.

Conversation with God, just like conversation with a friend, cements your relationship and makes you feel loved, encouraged and connected. But prayer to the Almighty Creator of the universe does more than provide warm fuzzies. Prayer moves the hand of God. We read in James 5:16 that "the prayer of a righteous person is powerful and effective." Prayer changes things. Prayer changes *us*.

# Why Should We Pray?

We pray because God hears and responds to our prayers. If you were to peek inside my Bible, you would see several underlined verses. I've drawn a big, bold star next to one passage in particular. Here it is:

> I love the LORD because he hears my voice
>> and my prayer for mercy.
> Because he bends down to listen,
>> I will pray as long as I have breath! (Ps. 116:1-2, *NLT*).

Pause and think for a moment about the truth revealed in Psalm 116. God isn't some far-off, impersonal deity. On the contrary, God knows the sound of your voice. He hears you when you pray. God bends down to listen to the cries of your heart.

When my children were young, occasionally I would feel a tug on my arm, accompanied by a tiny hand waving me to bend down so my child could whisper in my ear. As I stooped low, my child would cup his or her little fingers around my ear and whisper a need, a desire or some other piece of personal, intimate information. This, my sweet friend, is what God does for you and me. We are His children. He bends low to listen. We can cup our human hands around His divine ear and whisper our deepest needs, desires and longings to the one who loves us.

In Psalm 62, David encourages us with these words: "Trust in him at all times, you people; pour out your hearts to him, for God is our refuge" (Ps. 62:8). Because God listens to our voices and hears our prayers, we can trust Him with our most personal issues; we can pour out our hearts to Him. God is the trusted friend who not only listens, but who also has the power to intervene on our behalf. Prayer, then, makes sense. Therefore, "I will pray as long as I have breath."

All too commonly, though, our prayers can become nothing more than an afterthought—the "Oh yeah, God, it would be really great if You could bless what I already have in mind" variety. Some use prayer as a bargaining chip: "God, if You'll get me out of this mess, then I promise I'll serve the poor, give to charity, never do this again (you fill in the blank)." However, Scripture unearths a major key to authentic prayer: "Then you will call on me and come and pray to me, and I will listen to you. You will seek me and find me *when you seek me with all your heart*" (Jer. 29:12-13, emphasis added).

Prayer is not a last-ditch effort, only to be used when all else fails. Prayer is a whole-hearted search for God and His will. God listens to women who pray with seeking hearts. God responds to the gal who sincerely seeks to know God, who seeks to find God's purpose and discover God's plan. The bottom line is this: In prayer our heart becomes united with God's heart. A praying person is a seeking person.

We pray because we find God in prayer. We pray because we have a God who listens to our prayers, accepts our prayers and answers our prayers. We pray because our prayers are powerful and effective. We pray because our prayers please God.

MOST PEOPLE FOCUS ON THE PRAYER. GOD, HOWEVER, FOCUSES ON THE PRAY-ER.

## How Do We Pray?

Prayer was such an integral part of Jesus' life that His disciples asked Him to teach them to pray. Day after day, the 12 watched Jesus get up early, find a solitary spot and pray. Sometimes they observed Him pray throughout the night. Sometimes they watched Him pray at dawn. When they didn't know where to find Him, they almost always found Him praying. Jesus prayed so often that His followers longed to know what He knew about prayer. Luke 11:1-13 records Jesus' answer to their request, "Lord, teach us to pray" (v. 1). His teaching on prayer is also repeated in Matthew 6, as part of one of His most famous sermons, sometimes called "The Sermon on the Mount."

Jesus went to great lengths to help people understand prayer as an overflow of the heart. Read for yourself what Jesus had to say about prayer:

> And when you pray, do not be like the hypocrites, for they love to pray standing in the synagogues and on the street corners to be seen by others. Truly I tell you, they have received their reward in full. But when you pray, go into your room, close the door and pray to your Father, who is unseen. Then your Father, who sees what is done in secret, will reward you. And when you pray, do not keep on babbling like pagans, for they think they will be heard because of their many words. Do not be like them, for your Father knows what you need before you ask him. This, then, is how you should pray: "Our Father in heaven, hallowed be your name, your kingdom come, your will be done, on earth as it is in heaven. Give us today our daily bread. And forgive us our debts, as we also have forgiven our debtors. And lead us not into temptation, but deliver us from the evil one" (Matt. 6:5-13).

In His enlightening teaching on prayer, Jesus gives two don't do this and one do this. Jesus warns against praying to be noticed by others, and He warns against meaningless repetition. In other words, it's not people who use big religious-sounding words or words their hearts have no connection to that God hears. Rather, God responds to the sincere, intimate prayer of a person who talks to God from the depths of her soul. Prayer is not a matter of the words we speak; prayer is an overflow of the heart, which is ironic since most people focus on the prayer; God, however, focuses on the pray-er.

Jesus reinforces this concept when He states the prayer "do": "But when you pray, go into your room, close the door and pray to your Father, who is unseen. Then your Father, who sees what is done in secret, will reward you." Why would Jesus encourage private prayer? Because what you do when no one else is watching reveals the true state of your heart. Only a sincere God-seeker prays when no one but God sees.

---

WHAT YOU DO WHEN NO ONE ELSE IS
WATCHING REVEALS THE TRUE STATE OF YOUR
HEART. ONLY A SINCERE GOD-SEEKER PRAYS WHEN
NO ONE BUT GOD SEES.

---

Jesus promises that God rewards those who pray with sincere hearts. He also explains how we are to pray in what's commonly known as the Lord's Prayer. This prayer isn't to be used as a rote prayer (remember what Jesus warned about meaningless repetition) but rather as a model prayer. Jesus says this is *how* you should pray, not *what* you should pray. Why doesn't Jesus tell us what to pray? Because prayer isn't about the words; it's about the heart.

# The Elements of Prayer

Jesus' model prayer does help us understand the elements of prayer. For starters, prayer is addressed to our heavenly Father. A father is one who lovingly protects and provides for His children. When we pray to our Father in heaven, we acknowledge that God is big enough, strong enough and loving enough to protect us and provide for us. You may or may not have had an earthly father who protected and provided for you. You do, however, have a heavenly Father who can and will protect you and provide for you. Your heavenly Father can give you guidance when you are confused. He can work on your behalf. He can heal your body, your mind and your soul. Once a woman meets God through a relationship with Jesus Christ, she is ushered into an intimacy with God not known beforehand. That intimacy is reflected in knowing God as her loving heavenly Father, whom she can access through prayer.

The next line, "hallowed be thy name," may seem a bit confusing for those not raised in the Christian tradition. "Hallowed" simply means "honored." In other words, when we pray, we are to ask God to be honored by what we are requesting. To honor God in our prayers, we praise God for who He is and what He has done. In my personal prayer life, I often begin my prayers by recounting God's attributes, saying something like, "God, thank You that You love me, that You hear me and that You are in control of the whole universe. You are powerful and compassionate and caring." When I pause to remember who I am praying *to*, what I am praying *for* gets placed in perspective.

This idea is further addressed in the next line of the prayer, "your kingdom come, your will be done on earth as it is in heaven." In other words, we are to ask for God's good and perfect plan above our own selfish agendas. When we pray according to God's will, we can have tremendous confidence that God will answer our prayer. We read in 1 John 5:14-15, "This is the confidence we have in approaching God: that if we ask anything according to his will, he hears us. And if we know that he hears us—whatever we ask—we know that we have what we asked of him." If praying according to God's will gets results, the million-dollar question then becomes, "How can I make sure I am praying according to God's will?" Simple. When what you pray for aligns with what God has revealed in His Word, the Bible, you are praying according to His will.

Jesus promised, "If you remain in me and my words remain in you, ask whatever you wish, and it will be done for you" (John 15:7). When your prayers reflect the purposes and priorities of God, you can be confident that God will respond. The apostle James further explained the importance of praying rightly: "You do not have because you do not ask God. When you ask, you do not receive, because you ask with wrong motives" (Jas. 4:2-3).

Does this mean you can never ask God for anything other than something "spiritual"? Does this mean you shouldn't ask God to help you find a job, or sell your house, or figure out which college to attend? Not at all. In fact, the next line of Jesus' prayer assures us that we can ask God to provide for our needs. He tells us to pray "Give us this day our daily bread." God invites us to ask Him to meet our needs, whether those needs are physical, mental, social or spiritual.

Sometimes our needs are practical, like money to pay our bills. Sometimes our needs are less tangible, like wisdom to raise our kids. Sometimes our needs are emotional, like comfort for a grieving heart. God invites us to bring our whole selves to Him in prayer. Because He is our loving heavenly Father, we can talk to Him about anything and everything.

I was one of those "does she ever stop talking" children. I can remember coming home after school and spouting off endless details about my day, my friendship dramas, my boy-friend dilemmas and my childish hopes and dreams. My sweet mom patiently listened with interest to every word. As I grew older, it dawned on me how meaningless my idle chatter must have seemed to her. I mean, seriously, did my mom really care that the cute boy in math class didn't know I existed? Why was she always so interested in things that must have seemed trivial to her? So, I asked her. I'll never forget her answer: "Honey, if it's important to you, it's important to me."

God's heart for you echoes my mom's heart for me. If some-thing is important to you, it's important to God. Because He is your loving heavenly parent, your concerns are His concerns. Your needs are His needs. Your burdens are His burdens. Your heartaches are His heartaches. Your joys are His joys. Because God cares for you, He invites you to "cast all your anxiety on him" (1 Pet. 5:7). He invites you to ask, "give us this day, our daily bread," whatever that daily bread might be.

Jesus also teaches us to ask God for forgiveness ("forgive us of our debts") and to ask for strength to resist temptation ("lead us not into temptation, but deliver us from the evil one"). Our con-versations with God involve righting wrongs through confession to Him and asking for the strength to resist future temptation. In other words, we should pray for our character as much as we pray for our concerns. Prayer is not only about getting things from God. Prayer is also about becoming someone for God.

When our son, Taylor, was just three years old, he began praying a simple prayer when we tucked him into bed each night. With his hands folded and his eyes shut tight, we'd hear him whisper in the darkness, "God, thank You for the world and my family. Help me to be brave, strong and courageous." No doubt he began praying this prayer because he heard his dad pray these words for him. In fact, when Taylor was born, my husband chose Joshua 1:9—"Be strong and courageous. Do not be afraid"—to pray for him every day.

During middle school Taylor came home from church camp and added a new line to his prayer: "and may people know I'm a Christian by my actions." To this day, I have no idea what transpired at that weekend camp, though it soon became obvious that whatever happened changed his prayers. Taylor is now a young adult who is indeed brave, strong and courageous. If you met him, you'd be struck by one overriding characteristic—you would know he is a Christian by his actions.

As a young child, as a teenager, and now as a young adult, my son has consistently prayed that he would become the kind of person God wants him to be. When God invites us into prayer, he invites us to participate in seeing Him at work. Sometimes God works in our circumstances; sometimes God works in us. That's the miracle of prayer.

## What About Unanswered Prayer?

Prayer is easy enough for a child to understand, but deep enough to confound theologians. Nearly every praying person can cite an example of unanswered prayer. There are times when God doesn't seem to answer our prayers—or at least He doesn't answer the way we hoped and prayed He would. When we don't see immediate answers, we can be prone to discouragement, disillusionment and even disbelief. *Why doesn't God answer my prayers? Is something wrong with me? Is something wrong with God? What's the deal?*

It's been said that God answers prayer in one of three ways: yes; not yet; or no, because I love you too much.

As a parent, I can relate to these responses. If my child asks for something that is in her best interests, I say yes. Sometimes, though, one of my kids asks for something he or she isn't quite ready for—yet. It's not that I want to say no; it's just that the timing isn't right. Then there are times when the most loving thing I can do for my child is to say no. Rarely do my children understand my no answers in the heat of the moment. To them, my no seems unreasonable or even uncaring. Nothing could be further from the truth. I say no because what they have asked for is simply not the best for them, or because they need an attitude adjustment in order to appreciate a yes, or because I have something better planned.

One thing is certain though: My response is motivated by love. And so is God's.

Always.

The Bible gives us several reasons for unanswered prayer, including unbelief, harboring unforgiveness, selfish motives and sinful behavior. To understand prayer, we must never forget that God deals first and foremost with our hearts. When your heart isn't right because of an attitude or an action, God sometimes withholds His answer until your life dovetails with His. As a parent, I get this. If my child asks for something with a sense of ungrateful entitlement, rarely do I give it. It's not that I want to say no, or that I want to punish my child; my motive for not granting a selfish demand from a rebellious child relates to his or her character, not his or her request. Saying yes to a child like this only reinforces negative actions and attitudes.

In the same way, God—our loving, wise, heavenly Father—sometimes withholds answering our prayers not because He can't answer, or because He won't answer, but because He is forging our character. He's waiting for us to face up to our stuff, ask for forgiveness and get back on track. Let's be honest—if our attitudes and actions are filled with sin, how likely is it that our prayers are going to reflect right priorities and pure motives?

Sometimes our prayers go unanswered because of our own attitudes or actions.

But not always. Sometimes our prayers go unanswered for other reasons. Frankly, sometimes we don't know why God says no. Should that stop us from praying?

Jesus addressed this question head-on. He told His followers to pray and not give up. Prayer isn't some kind of good luck arrow you shoot up to God in your time of need and forget you prayed two seconds later. Prayer is an ongoing relational conversation with God. And although we don't like it, sometimes God makes us wait. What are we to do when God doesn't answer our prayers right away? We can throw up our hands in despair and quit, or we can keep praying.

> PRAYER ISN'T ONLY ABOUT GETTING
> THINGS FROM GOD. PRAYER IS ALSO ABOUT
> BECOMING SOMEONE FOR GOD.

## When God Says Wait

Almost exactly one year ago today our family began to see the answer to a prayer that took 40 years to answer. In case you skimmed right over that last sentence, let me repeat the time frame—40 years. Not 40 minutes. Not 40 days. Not even 40 months. Forty *years*.

Forty years ago, my brother-in-law became the very first Christian in his family. As the first believer, he began praying for his family members every day. Specifically, he prayed that they would each come to faith. After several years and a few awkward conversations, my husband followed his brother's footsteps and became a Christian. They both began to pray for their mom and stepdad. Every day. Was it discouraging at times? You bet. Did they ever give up hope? Yep, especially when they were told, "Please don't talk to us about God anymore." Respectfully, they stopped talking about God, but they never stopped praying. Or loving. Or visiting, or calling or caring.

For 40 years.

About this time last year, my mother-in-law shocked us by announcing that she was considering going to church "just to see." We held our breath and continued to pray. She went and liked it. Several women invited her to lunch. These women were warm, thoughtful, even downright normal, and my mother-in-law liked them immediately. They invited her to join their home Bible study. She went "just to see." She liked that too. Soon she signed up to be a Sunday morning greeter at church. Six months ago, she called my husband to ask, "How do I become a Christian, exactly? I've been waiting for someone at church to tell me, but they never do."

Why did it take 40 years of prayer before my wonderful mother-in-law made a spiritual commitment? Honestly, I have no idea. Sometimes we just don't know why God works the way He does. What I do know is this: We're glad we didn't stop praying, even if it took 40 years to see the answer.

Maybe you've prayed for something to happen that is near and dear to your heart but have yet to see God answer. Perhaps you're tempted to give up. You might even be toying with thoughts about how God doesn't hear your prayers or care about your concerns. It's easy to give up when we don't see immediate results. The enemy would like nothing more than to sideline you and your prayers. Don't let the enemy win. Keep on praying, and don't stop . . . *even if it takes 40 years to see the answer.*

# When God Says No

It's one thing to endure in prayer when God makes you wait, but it's another thing altogether when God tells you no outright. No is a bitter pill to swallow if we fail to see the loving hand it's sifted through. When God says no, it's easy to be angry with Him. Or we become discouraged, disillusioned or disbelieving. It's easy to buy into the lie that God doesn't love you as much as He loves other people. Or maybe you even start to wonder if God exists at all.

It's easy to lose faith.

You may have never considered this before, but Jesus received a no to one of His prayers. Mark 14:32-42 records Jesus' prayer the night before His crucifixion. Deeply troubled and distressed, Jesus asked the Father, "Take this cup from me" (v. 36), begging for an alternative to the cross. In essence Jesus said, "Father, if Your plan for salvation can be accomplished in any other way, please do it. I don't want to be crucified."

Does it surprise you that Jesus felt troubled and distressed? Does it shock you that Jesus didn't want to be crucified? To die by crucifixion meant the most painful, horrific death a human being could experience. In His humanity, Christ asked for another way.

Ultimately, though, Jesus was willing to do whatever the Father deemed necessary. "Yet not what I will, but what you will" (Mark 14:36). Three times Jesus unloaded His heartfelt plea for the Father to remove the cup of sacrifice from Him. Finally, though, the answer came.

No.

Jesus knows what it's like to pour your heart out to the Father, begging for an escape from a horrific circumstance. He also knows how it feels to ask but not receive the answer you hoped for. Most importantly, He knows how God's no, though painful at the moment, is always filtered through the hands of love—

love for us and for those around us. That's why Jesus could pray, "Yet not my will, but your will be done." Jesus asked if there was any way possible to be spared from dying a sacrificial death on a cross. God said no. God's no, however, led to the ultimate *yes*.

Yes to salvation for millions. Yes to eternal glory for Christ. Yes to resurrection life. Yes to victory over death. Yes to the defeat of sin. Yes to God's eternal plan. Yes to life everlasting.

One *no* meant a thousand wonderful *yeses*.

And so it is with you and me. When we pray, God hears and answers. Sometimes He says yes. Sometimes He says not yet. Sometimes He says no. But make no mistake—prayer always moves the hand of God. The answer will result in His glory, the benefit of others and our ultimate good.

What should you do when God says no? Remember Jesus. Remember how God turned one no into a thousand yeses. Remember God's character—that He is always good, always loving and always wise, even if it doesn't *feel* like it in the moment. Remember that His ways are not always our ways. Remember that He sees the beginning from the end and knows the whole story, while we see only part of it. Remember that God will never leave you or forsake you. Remember that if you know Christ as your Savior, you are God's child and He has your best interests at heart. Always.

Prayer is conversation with God. The more you talk to Him and allow Him to talk to you, the deeper your relationship will become. God loves you; He wants to spend time with you talking about your life, your concerns, your needs and your struggles. God wants you to pray for yourself and those around you. He bends down to listen. He hears and He answers. When God says yes, thank Him. When God says wait, trust Him. When God says no, depend on Him.

And keep praying as long as you have breath.

# For Further Study

Up to this point in your life, what has been your perspective on prayer?

According to the following verses, why should we pray?

Psalm 6:9

Psalm 116:1-2

Jeremiah 29:11-13

James 5:16

The prayer recorded in Matthew 6:9-13 is often referred to as the Lord's Prayer. Have you ever heard anyone recite the Lord's Prayer without really considering its meaning? Have you ever been guilty of doing this? How does praying a rote prayer, without sincerity of heart, relate to Jesus' warning in Matthew 6:5-7 not to pray to be heard by men or babble meaninglessly?

What did Jesus tell us about prayer, according to the passages below?

Matthew 21:22

Mark 11:25

Luke 18:1-7

Why do you think faith, forgiveness and perseverance are key components to prayer?

Jesus taught that we are to pray believing God. God hears the cries of our heart. He knows every spoken and unspoken prayer. But sometimes our prayers seem to go unanswered. Why is this? How does the Bible address this dilemma?

Read the following verses and note any factor that can hinder our prayers:

Psalm 66:18

Matthew 6:5

James 1:6-7

James 4:2-3

Did any of the hindrances to prayer surprise you? What new insight did you learn about unanswered prayer?

It's been said that God answers prayer in one of three ways: (1) yes; (2) not yet; or (3) no, because I love you too much. You may have never considered this before, but Jesus received a no to one of His prayers. Mark 14:32-42 records Jesus' prayer the night before His crucifixion. After reading the words of His prayer, answer the following: (Note: Reading Mark 14 in its entirety will give you a better picture of the events that took place the night before Jesus died. If you have time, read all of Mark 14.)

How did Jesus feel?

What did Jesus ask?

Ultimately, what did Jesus want?

_____

_____

_____

After praying three times, what did Jesus do?

_____

_____

Read the following passages and list things we are encouraged
to pray for:

Psalm 90:12

_____

_____

_____

Psalm 90:17

_____

_____

_____

Ephesians 1:16-18

_____

_____

_____

Ephesians 3:14-21

_____

_____

_____

Ephesians 6:18-20

1 Timothy 2:1-3

Hebrews 4:16

James 5:13-14

Which of these passages was most meaningful to you? Why?

When are we to pray?

Psalm 55:16-17

Philippians 4:6

1 Thessalonians 5:16-18

At times we may find ourselves in circumstances where we don't know how to pray or what to pray. In moments like these, what does God do for us through His Spirit, according to Romans 8:26?

# 9

# Attitudes Count

Last night, JP and I attended a party where we found ourselves embroiled in a funny but telling conversation. As it turns out, some of our friends consider themselves rule followers, and some of our friends don't. I guess this should come as no surprise. Poke your head into any elementary, middle school or high school classroom and right away you'll spot the rule followers—the kid who always raises her hand; the child who tattles on kids who cut in line; the student who would never, ever, consider turning in a late homework assignment.

Then there are those who push the envelope. Rules, they figure, are more like "guidelines" than specific instructions to follow to the letter. If a rule makes sense to them, or if they personally benefit by following a rule, they're all in. But if a rule seems arbitrary or inconvenient, forget it. These are the kids who turn in homework when it suits them; the ones who pay attention in class only when they are interested in the subject matter; the ones who come home before curfew only if nothing better is going on. You know what I am talking about, because you know these kids. Heck, we *are* these kids. Like JP's and my friends, we all fall somewhere along the continuum of these two camps. We either lean toward being a rule follower or tend to push the limits. To complicate matters, and depending on circumstances, sometimes we can be both.

Last month I flew home from a speaking engagement and was seated next to an acne-faced, highly accomplished teenager and a 20-something gal wearing cute boots who was uncertain about what she wanted to do in life. In other words, pretty typical people. Being seated next to these two strangers turned out to be an interesting study in human behavior.

A few minutes before departure, the flight attendant announced that it was time to turn off all electronic equipment. My row-mates both ignored the announcement. Later, the flight attendant walked down the aisle, again reminding passengers to turn off all cell phones. I feigned interest in my magazine but couldn't help notice them both ignore the request once more. Finally, the flight attendant spoke with each of them personally. They nodded compliance but hid their still active cell phones underneath their coats and blankets.

Their behavior piqued my curiosity. *Why don't they simply turn off their cell phones?* I wondered. Looking back, I probably should have minded my own business, but in the moment, their actions intrigued me. I just couldn't resist. I had to ask.

"You're not going to be one of those people who act like our mother, are you?" they responded, feeling irritated and entitled. Now I wasn't merely curious, I was bugged. I bit my tongue and looked back at my magazine, resisting the temptation to comment; instead I replayed the scene in my mind. Why did they behave the way they did? Why did I?

Clearly we fell on different sides of the rule-follower/rule-breaker spectrum (I guess you don't have to guess which one I am). But here's the kicker—both our responses were simply differing symptoms of the same disease—pride. Stay with me while I explain why.

Biblically speaking, "pride" differs from being excited about achieving an accomplishment or being proud of a success: *I feel proud that I resisted the brownie; I'm proud of my teenager for not bending to peer pressure; I'm proud that I worked hard enough to earn the promotion; I'm proud that I persevered to achieve a goal.* These examples are not the same thing as having the kind of prideful attitude the Bible speaks of. Feeling proud of an accomplishment is normal and good and is necessary for sound mental health. The type of pride that reared its ugly head at 30,000 feet in the air occurs when we have an excessively high opinion of ourselves or a low opinion of others. Unhealthy pride shows up in conceit, arrogance or a condescending attitude, and it exhibits itself in one of two primary ways—rebellious actions or judgmental attitudes—and, sometimes, both.

This kind of pride caused my fellow passengers to ignore instructions. This kind of pride caused me to butt in. They rebelled, considering themselves above the rules; I judged, considering myself above the people seated next to me.

This isn't to say that some things are right and some things are wrong. They are. But I'm referring to the state of the heart. What's in our hearts affects how we behave, how we think and how we live more than most of us realize. Pride, in its worst form, causes us to live as if we're the center of the universe. A person who's self-centered has little room to be others-centered, much less God-centered.

My great-grandmother used to call prideful people "full of themselves." She'd remind her children about the dangers of pride with her pithy, homespun saying: "If you get too big for your britches, the Lord will have to split them." Why is pride such a big deal? It's destructive. My great-grandmother's years of wisdom taught her that unhealthy, self-centered pride topples more marriages, friendships, businesses, governments and individual lives than all other vices combined.

Because of its destructive nature, God deals harshly with prideful people: "God opposes the proud but shows favor to the humble" (1 Pet. 5:5). I don't know about you, but if there's one being I don't want opposing me, it's God. Pride is the roadblock that detours our journey toward God. A prideful person can't find God, because meeting God takes a giant dose of humility. Pride is the single factor that can thwart our capacity to meet God.

Let that thought sink in for a minute.

The only thing that can stop you from meeting God is self-centered pride. Not your mistakes, stupid choices or a sordid past. Not your lack of knowledge about God. Not your background or your age or your religious predispositions. Nothing can stop a person from meeting God except pride, because pride makes "self" God.

Pride says, *I'm a really good person—at least as good as most, and probably better than many—and my life is just fine without God.* Translation: *You pitiful thing. Too bad you are so weak that you need God. If you were as together as I am, you wouldn't.*

Pride mockingly says, *Believing in God is belief in a fairy tale. You can't really know if God exists.* Translation: *I don't believe, and since I know everything (or think I do), anyone who differs from me is an idiot.*

Pride declares, *If Christianity works for you, great. But don't push your beliefs on me.* Translation: *I'll make up my own rules of right and wrong according to how I see fit. I'd like to be my own God, thank you very much.*

Pride says, *The God that I believe in would never allow evil or suffering in the world. The God of the Bible is mean, and I don't like that God.* Translation: *I'll only believe in a God of my own making; one that I can manage and who does only what makes sense to me.*

Can you relate to any of these statements? My guess is that you've never considered these attitudes a stumbling block to meeting God. But they are. Prideful people place themselves on the throne—the place that only God deserves. Is it any wonder that in order to meet God, we must humble ourselves and relinquish our pride? And boy, oh boy, can this be hard.

Most of us don't like to be told what to do. We like to be masters of our own fate. In fact, sometimes we're even bugged that we're expected to follow the rules (even God's). But what's even more telling is that we're bugged when other people don't follow the rules. Need proof? The last time you observed someone speeding down the highway, what did you think when he or she zipped by you? Probably something like, *What a jerk!* Right?

But do you ever speed? (Do I even have to ask?)

What makes us this way? We are rule followers one day and rule breakers the next. We're judgmental of others' behavior, but we're blinded to the inequity of our own. We behave like this because we're all infected with the disease of pride. We either do what we want to do, when we want to do it, or we judge others who don't behave like we think they should.

Pride affects the way we view life, ourselves, other people and God.

Jesus told a story about two men who came to the temple to pray. One was a religious man, the other a guy who'd lived life on his own terms without thought of God—until this moment. One considered God lucky to have him on His side, while the other didn't even have the nerve to look up toward heaven. I love their story, and I think you will too.

To some who were confident of their own righteousness and looked down on everyone else, Jesus told this parable: "Two men went up to the temple to pray, one a Pharisee and the other a tax collector. The Pharisee stood by himself and prayed: 'God, I thank you that

I am not like other people—robbers, evildoers, adulterers—or even like this tax collector. I fast twice a week and give a tenth of all I get.' But the tax collector stood at a distance. He would not even look up to heaven, but beat his breast and said, 'God, have mercy on me, a sinner.' I tell you that this man, rather than the other, went home justified before God. For all those who exalt themselves will be humbled, and those who humble themselves will be exalted" (Luke 18:9-14).

This is the classic good guy/bad guy story, except that the good guy here turns out to be the bad guy, and the bad guy turns out to be the good guy. Why? Because when the two men stood praying before God, one man was prideful while the other man was humble. One was full of self, but the other was emptied of self. One had a high view of his own righteousness; the other had a high view of God.

How does Jesus comment on these two individuals? Go back and reread Jesus' words again. They are powerful.

"I tell you that this man [the one who humbly asked for mercy] went home justified before God."

Do you want to be in a right relationship with God? You don't have to be perfect. You don't have to be religious. You don't have to have all the answers.

But you do have to be humble.

Everyone who exalts herself will be humbled—if not in this life, in the life to come. You can count on it. But just as surely, every person who humbles herself before God will be exalted. In other words, God lifts up those who bend down before Him. Is it easy to push your pride aside and humble yourself before God? No. In fact, humbling oneself before God can be painful, difficult and even scary.

We might fight God for years before we finally relinquish our pride and turn to Him. True humility doesn't come easily for any of us. However, you might be interested to know that God never requires something of us that He doesn't model Himself.

As I type these words, it's 2:00 PM on Christmas Eve. In a few hours our family will gather at church for Christmas Eve services. Tomorrow we will celebrate the birth of Christ. Of course, there will be presents under the tree, family gathered together, lots of noise and even more food. But the crux of Christmas is one history-altering event: God humbled Himself to live among us. His birth didn't occur in a top-notch medical facility, but rather in a smelly stable where He was laid in a feeding trough (in case you've ever wondered what a manger is, now you know). The Creator of the universe humbled Himself by taking the form of a lowly infant born to an unknown Jewish couple, in a remote village in the Middle East. Picture yourself becoming an ant and you'll get the picture of what God did that first Christmas day. God became flesh and lived among us.

Not above us.

Among us.

With us.

Humility personified.

God humbled Himself so that we could know Him; all He asks is that we do the same. The only thing that can stop us from knowing God is our unwillingness to surrender our self-focused pride.

## What Is Humility, Anyway?

Humility has gotten a bad rap. Most people think of humility as a negative quality, equating it with being spineless, frail or impotent. Humility seems weak. And we don't like weak. We like strong. We like independent. We like control. Our culture values the movers and shakers of the world, the men and women who push their way to the top. The divas. The powerful. The superstars. The rich and famous. But the humble? Well, bless their hearts, we hope they'll somehow get by.

Although humility is often associated with weakness, nothing could be further from the truth. Because we are naturally inclined toward pride, humbling oneself takes tremendous strength. I've heard it said that the job of humility isn't to make us feel small, but to expand our capacity for appreciation and awe; to enable us to stand silent before all that we do not know and then to get on with the work of finding out. *Webster's* defines humility as "the quality or state of not thinking you are better than other people." According to Yourdictionary.com, "humble describes someone who knows they are not perfect."

Can you see why humility is necessary in order to meet God? A person who thinks she is perfect will never see her need for God. Such a person finds herself looking down on others . . . and you can't look up when you're too busy looking down.

This can be a tough pill to swallow. Even Jesus' followers had trouble understanding the necessity of humility. Like us, they wanted to climb the ladder of success. They wanted to be top dog; famous; esteemed. So they asked Jesus how to do it. They didn't tap-dance around the subject. They cut to the core of the issue and asked Christ bluntly.

> About that time the disciples came to Jesus and asked, "Who is greatest in the Kingdom of Heaven?" Jesus called a little child to him and put the child among them. Then he said, "I tell you the truth, unless you turn from your sins and become like little children, you will never get into the Kingdom of Heaven. So anyone

who becomes as humble as this little child is the greatest in the Kingdom of Heaven" (Matt. 18:1-4, *NLT*).

Jesus answered their question just as directly as they asked
it. Who is greatest? "The person who becomes humble." In
God's economy, the way up is down.

C. S. Lewis, acclaimed scholar at Oxford University, and
author of *The Chronicles of Narnia* and *Mere Christianity* among
other great works, wrote this about his own journey of faith: "I
gave in, and admitted that God was God." In its simplest form,
the essence of humility is acknowledging that God is God, and
we are not.

---

### You can't look up when you're too busy looking down.

---

Make no mistake; humility takes guts. It's easier to ignore
God than embrace Him. It's easier to let God's Word fall on
deaf ears than to heed it. It's easier to push our own agenda
than submit to someone else's. It's easier to break the rules
than follow them. It's easier to take all the credit than share the
glory. It's easier to justify selfishness than just admit self-cen-
teredness. Humility isn't easy, and it certainly doesn't always
come naturally, but the payoff of trading a prideful attitude
for a humble one is big. It pays off in unified relationships,
reconciled families, healthy work environments and meeting
God. In fact, God declares:

> These are the ones I look on with favor: those who are
> humble and contrite in spirit, and who tremble at my
> word (Isa. 66:2).

God esteems—He respects, notices, accepts, welcomes—the woman who is humble and contrite in her heart.

You know what? So do we.

Would you rather be in a relationship with someone who is self-focused or others-centered? Would you rather work with someone who is a team player or a backstabber? Would you rather converse with someone who talks only about herself or listens to you? Would you rather parent a child who accepts correction or rebels against it?

The answer, of course, is that we would rather surround ourselves with humble people. We understand the havoc pride brings. We're repulsed by prideful personalities. And yet, there isn't a person among us who doesn't struggle with pride in some form. C. S. Lewis put it this way:

> There is one vice in which no man in the world is free, which every man in the world loathes when he sees it in someone else, and of which hardly any people, except Christians, ever imagine they are guilty themselves. I have heard people admit they are bad-tempered, or they cannot keep their heads about girls, or drink, or even that they are cowards. I do not think I have ever heard anyone who was not a Christian accuse himself of this vice. The vice I am talking about is pride.[1]

Pride is common to all people, yet self-apparent to few. However, if we want to meet God, it's imperative that we deal with our pride head-on. As I mentioned earlier in this chapter, pride is the single factor that can prevent you and me from meeting God. Humility is required. We must be willing to come to God on His terms, not our own. If we want to dictate the terms of our relationship to the Almighty, we can't know God. Meeting God just doesn't work that way. God is God; we are not.

He is infinite; we are finite.

He is the Creator; we are the created.

He gets to set the parameters for how human beings enter into a relationship with Him, not the other way around.

Does this sound harsh, narrow and mean? It's not. In fact, if you stop to think about it, the fact that we finite creatures even have the possibility of knowing our infinite Creator is mind blowing. Because God is love, He provides a way for us to meet Him, know Him and be in relationship with Him. All we have to do is humble ourselves long enough to find the path He's set for us to find Him, then follow it.

This means we'll have to do things God's way, even if we're naturally inclined to be rule breakers. And it means we'll have to stop thinking of ourselves as better than others, especially if we lean toward being rule followers. There is simply no place for pride when a woman finds herself in the presence of God. God is opposed to the proud.

But God gives grace to the humble.

# For Further Study

Read Luke 18:9-14 and answer the following questions:

With what kind of attitude did the religious person approach God?

What kind of attitude did the tax collector have?

Which man did Jesus commend?

What surprises you or impresses you about this story?

How does this story encourage you?

How does this story convict you?

According to the following verses, what kinds of attitudes are necessary to enter into the presence of God?

Psalm 51:17

Isaiah 57:15

Isaiah 66:2

Matthew 18:1-4

When we come to God with a contrite spirit—a heart that's sorry, remorseful and repentant—God welcomes us into His presence. This kind of attitude requires humility. Read Matthew 23:11-13 and 1 Peter 5:5-7.

What do these verses tell us about God's upside-down economy?

What attitude is the opposite of humility?

How does God respond to the proud?

According to the following Scripture, what other attitudes are necessary in order to meet God?

Psalm 42:2

Isaiah 55:1-2

John 7:37

Matthew 11:28

Humility and obedience go hand in hand. Read Philippians 2:5-11. How did Christ model humility? With what result?

Now read Philippians 2:3-5. According to these verses, how are we to follow Christ's example?

According to the following verses, what is the relationship between our love for God and our obedience to Him?

Deuteronomy 11:1

John 14:23

What are the benefits of obeying God?

Joshua 1:7-8

Jeremiah 7:22-24

Even though God's commands and laws are given with our best interests in mind, we sometimes still find it difficult to obey. Why do you think this is so?

People have a host of reasons or excuses for why they choose to do their own thing rather than what God wants them to do. Put a check beside any of the reasons listed below that have factored into your obedience or disobedience:

❑  I'm scared to do what God wants me to do.
❑  I don't know what God wants me to do.
❑  I don't care what God wants me to do.
❑  I think I know what's best for my life, so why ask God?
❑  I'll do part of what God wants me to do.
❑  God's commands don't make sense to me.
❑  God's commands seem too hard to keep.
❑  Following God's ways would make my life boring.

Which of these reasons have been the most influential in your life up to this point?

Would you like that to change? If yes, how?

God's laws are sometimes called precepts, ordinances, commands, instructions or decrees. Obedience to God's instruction is both a choice and a learned response. We decide to obey or to disobey. If we obey, God is pleased and we are blessed. If we don't, sooner or later we bear the consequences.

The psalmist (King David wrote most of the book of Psalms) asked God for help in following God's laws. According to Psalm 119:33-35, what did David pray?

How can asking for God's help to obey His Word encourage you in your life this week? Is there an area in which you need God's help? If so, write out a short prayer asking God to enable you to do what He wants you to do.

**Note**
1. C. S. Lewis, *Mere Christianity* (New York: Macmillan/Collier, 1955).

# The Really, Really Good News

What's the best news you ever received?

"Congratulations, you got the job."

"Good news—you're pregnant."

"It's not cancer."

"Your offer was accepted—the house is yours."

"I'm okay, Mom."

In a world filled with bad news, every one of us longs for good news. Bad news day after day, week after week, leaves us depleted, discouraged and hopeless. Maybe you've found yourself in a season of life where you've thought, *I just can't take one more negative thing. I can't hear one more piece of bad news, get one more discouraging report or experience one more heartbreaking rejection.* What you need is a little good news. God understands, and He has good news for you—great news, in fact.

No doubt you're familiar with the word "gospel," as in gospel choir or gospel music, or even just "the gospel." But did you know that "gospel" means "good news"? The message of God is straightforward. It can be boiled down into two words: good news.

What's so good about the good news? Simply this: God wants all people to know Him—including you. The God of the universe, maker of the heavens and earth, wants to have a relationship with *you*; He wants a friendship with *you*. God wants you to experience eternal life with Him in heaven; but He also wants you to experience abundant life with Him now. God wants *you* to live life forgiven and free. God wants *you* to experience every drop of His goodness and mercy and love. God wants *you* to know the purpose for which He created you. He wants *you* to live that purpose to its fullest potential.

God wants *you* to know *Him*.

Stop and let that sink in. Pause for a moment and allow your soul to drink in the magnitude of this truth. Can you see why this is good news? This news changes *everything*—your perspective on life, your relationships with others, your values and goals, your eternal destiny.

If God wants all people to know Him, why do so few people *really* know Him? The problem isn't with God; it's with us. We are our own worst enemy. Some people don't have a desire to know God. Some don't know how. Some people become preoccupied with other pursuits and prioritize meeting God on an invisible "Things I'll Do Someday" list they file somewhere in a remote part of their brain. Whatever the reason, we all live separate from God and would continue to do so if not for God's initiative toward us.

God created human beings to live in perfect communion with Him; but when Adam and Eve chose to disobey God, sin entered the world. Though they once enjoyed perfect friendship with God and unhindered relationship with one another, now they began to blame. They felt shame. They hid from God.

People have struggled with blame, shame and hiding from one another and God ever since. Sin has infiltrated the way we think, the way we feel and the way we behave.

The first man and woman, ashamed and embarrassed, expected to receive condemnation for their sin. Instead they received mercy. However, sin left its ugly image on them and on every man and woman to come after. Sin—failing God's standard of perfect holiness and righteousness—causes a gap between God and us. God is holy, and we are not. A huge chasm separates us from God, much like two friends who get caught on opposite sides of a washed-out bridge. Sin was the tidal wave that destroyed the bridge of perfect communion man was originally created to experience with God. "Surely the arm of the LORD is not too short to save, nor his ear to dull to hear. But your sins have separated you from your God" (Isa. 59:1-2).

The Bible is clear on the fact that our sin separates us from God. But even without the biblical explanation, we know it intuitively. Need proof? The last time you did something you were ashamed of, did you feel like opening your Bible or praying afterward? Would you want God sitting beside you as you did it? Doubtful. Why not? Sin causes us to hide from God.

Sin is the root cause of mankind's separation from God. Let me pause here and explain why it's imperative to understand the gravity of sin and its consequences. Let's suppose your best friend separates from her husband, who is also your friend. When you ask why, you're told they're separating because of his infidelity. Of course you're heartbroken for your dear friends.

A few days later you learn that they have decided to pursue marriage counseling. You are thrilled with the news and hopeful that the couple can be reconciled. Your hopes soar when you hear they are both faithfully attending therapy together twice a week. They seem to be on the road to restoration.

You're shocked when your friend announces she's decided to divorce her husband. "What went wrong?" you ask. "He seemed committed to make the marriage work." Only then does your friend reveal her husband's attitude during counseling. "When our therapist wanted us to deal with the issue of infidelity, he worked instead on bringing home a better salary, helping out more with the kids and finishing projects around the house. All those are good things, but they were never the cause of our separation. We couldn't be reconciled because he would never deal with the root cause of our problem."

What's true for a broken human relationship is also true for a broken relationship with God. For any relationship to be reconciled, the root cause of the separation must be addressed and dealt with. Any other solution isn't a solution at all.

What is the root cause of our separation from God? Sin. Therefore, to be reconciled with God, we must address the root issue of sin.

Sin causes a gap between man and God. Man's best effort at bridging the gap is called religion. Religion says, "Be good enough to be accepted." "Do this; don't do that." "Work your way to God." The difference between religion and Christianity is that religion is man's attempt to reach up to God, while Christianity is God reaching down to man. Religion is about rules; Christianity is about relationship. Religion says go to church, be baptized, volunteer, or any number of other "religious duties." While these are good things, they don't deal with the root issue. Becoming religious is as effective in reconciling a person to God as my friend's unfaithful husband's attempt to reconcile his marriage by helping more with household chores. Religion doesn't deal with the root cause of our separation from God any more than an unfaithful husband's willingness to do the laundry without ending an affair.

A religious person tries to clean up her sins; a Christian allows Christ to erase them.

# God's Part of the Equation

A few years ago, our middle daughter, Kylie, arrived home after the first day of a two-day cheer competition. The minute I saw her face, I asked, "What's wrong, honey?"

"Something happened, Mom, and I think you're going to be really, really mad."

*Uh-oh.*

She explained that after her team competed they had several hours before the awards ceremony. To make good use of the time, her coach took the girls on a tour of the *Queen Mary*—the ship where the competition was held. As Kylie walked up the steps of the ship, her cell phone slipped out of her jacket pocket. Panicked, she reached down to pick it up but she was too late—another tourist coming down the steps failed to see her phone and accidentally kicked it between the opening in the steps, landing her cell phone deep into the bowels of the *Queen Mary*.

"Are you mad, Mom?" she asked, her sweet face burdened with concern.

"Well, I'm kind of bummed, like you are, but I'm not mad. It was an accident that could have happened to anyone."

"Well," she continued hesitantly, "there's more."

*More? How could there be more?* I wondered.

Kylie went on to explain how hard she had tried to retrieve her cell phone, even calling a security guard over to the scene for assistance. In a last-ditch attempt to rescue the phone, Kylie took off her team jacket, knelt down onto the steps and thrust her arm between the stairs, struggling to stretch her arm far enough to reach the phone. All of her efforts proved useless. She was pretty sure her dad and I would be angry about the phone, but she really began to worry about our response when she saw her uniform sleeve after reaching between the greasy steps of a ship.

She slowly removed her jacket and held out her arm for me to see. Her once sparkling white uniform now bore an ugly black grease mark.

"I've ruined my uniform with the stain. Are you mad, Mom?"

I wasn't. However, I knew that stain had to be dealt with, and it had to be dealt with fast—the second day of Kylie's competition would start the next morning. I took the uniform from Kylie and began to do my laundry magic. I was convinced that with the right products and a little elbow grease I could have the black stain removed in no time at all.

I scrubbed. Then I soaked. Then I bleached. Then I scrubbed again, soaked again, bleached again and finally used the super-duper cleaning product that promises to take grease out of a driveway. The stain didn't budge. Though it seemed a bit fainter (at least I thought it did), the ugly back mark was visible for all to see. I began to worry. Maybe her stain would be permanent, after all.

Now it was late. Kylie had long gone to bed, but I was still running around the house like a mad woman, trying my best to get rid of that darn stain. JP plopped down on the sofa, picked up the remote control and began to watch a late-night movie. Noticing the dark circles under my eyes and my efforts to stifle bear-sized yawns, JP offered to deal with the stain himself.

I had to admit the offer was tempting. I was worn out, and he was her father, after all. How bad could it be if I left him a list of everything I would do if I were still awake? I succumbed, but not without writing detailed instructions on how to deal with the stain.

The next morning I awoke to find Kylie smiling from ear to ear, dressed in her pristine, sparkling white uniform. *Wow! Her dad is pretty amazing!* I thought. As I made breakfast, though, I began to notice an odd odor wafting through the air.

"Does anyone else smell that funny smell?" I asked our three kids who were seated at the breakfast table.

Yes, indeed, they smelled the odor. But, no, they had no idea what it could be. Just then, JP walked downstairs to join us.

"Do you happen to smell that funny smell?" I asked JP.

He sniffed deeply. "Oh . . . you mean that chemical smell?"

"Yeah, that's the one. What do you think it could be?'

"Oh, it's probably just Kylie."

"What? Why would our daughter smell like a chemical factory?"

"Well," JP said, "last night I tried all the techniques you left for me to get rid of the stain, and none of them worked. So I started thinking and came up with a plan—I spray painted her uniform, threw it in the dryer to set and, look, it's as white as snow!"

I had to admit that her stains were covered and her uniform looked perfect. I could never have predicted the lengths a father would go to cover the stains of his daughter!

What JP did for Kylie, God did for you and me.

We come to God, fearing His anger. "God, I'm stained. I'm ruined. Are You mad?"

Religion tells us that with the right "products"—a few good deeds, a little charity, church attendance, especially at Christmas and Easter, the right religious rituals and a little elbow grease, our stains will be removed. We work hard to be good people. Our stains seem to fade a bit; at least we think they do. But the stains are still there, visible for all to see. We yell at our family members. We lie. We make stupid choices. We refuse to forgive. We disobey God. All our efforts amount to nothing.

We exhaust ourselves by trying harder. But if we hand our stained lives over to our Father, He takes our stains—our sins—and covers them not with spray paint, but with the precious blood of Jesus. "'Come now, let us settle the matter,' says the LORD. 'Though your sins are like scarlet, they shall be white as

snow; though they are red as crimson, they shall be like wool"
(Isa. 1:18).

Through Christ's death and resurrection, our sins are
dealt with once for all. They are covered, removed, erased. Sin
requires a payment: "The wages of sin is death" (Rom. 6:23).
Christ died in our place, bearing the consequences for our sin.
Because of what Christ did for you and me—He covered our
stains—the chasm between God and man has been bridged.
Two who were separated can now be reconciled.

Only in Christ is sin—the real barrier between mankind and
God—adequately dealt with. No other religious leader or religion covers your sin. No philosophy does either. This is why
Jesus could boldly assert that He alone is the way to God: "No
one comes to the Father except through me" (John 14:6). Jesus
could say this because He alone removes the obstacle that separates us from God. Only God in the flesh loved you enough to
take your stained life and redeem it with His own.

This is the essential message of Christianity.

Christianity is not a religion; it's a relationship of love and
forgiveness and reconciliation. It's good news for those who
will accept it.

Think for a moment about the love it took for Jesus to willingly die in your place for your sins. It's one thing to bear the consequences of one's own wrongdoings; it's another thing altogether
to pay the debt for another's. What God did for you, in Christ, had
one motive—love. "God demonstrates his own love for us in this:
While we were still sinners, Christ died for us" (Rom. 5:8).

God loves us. God loves *you*. What you are, what you've
done, what you've believed, where you've come from, all of it is
irrelevant. God opens His arms wide for you.

One of the most well-known verses in the Bible further explains this concept: "For God so loved the world that he gave

his one and only Son, that whoever believes in him shall not perish but have eternal life" (John 3:16). The next verse tells us, "For God did not send his Son into the world to condemn the world, but to save the world through him" (v. 17).

## My Part of the Equation

God is the great pursuer of mankind. It seems kind of odd that more people don't respond. If someone famous pursued getting to know me, I'd be pretty thrilled. I mean, how cool would it be to be personal friends with your favorite actor? To have lunch with your favorite singer? To be invited to your favorite celebrity's home? Would you yawn and tell the person you'll have to think about it? Uh, no.

Yet this is what many of us do with God.

God offers an invitation. Jesus declares, "Come to me, all you who are weary and burdened, and I will give you rest" (Matt. 11:28). Notice that Jesus doesn't say, "Come to church, all you who are weary and burdened." Nor does He say, "Come to religion" or "Come to a philosophy" or "Come to spirituality." Jesus says plainly, "Come to *Me*." Christianity is about Christ. If you take Christ out of Christianity, you're left with nothing. A Christian is a Christ follower.

How, exactly, does one come to Christ? By faith. Remember John 3:16: "For God so loved the world that he gave his one and only Son, that whoever *believes* in him shall not perish but have eternal life" (emphasis added). Paul clarifies even further, "For it is by grace you have been saved, *through faith*—and this is not from yourselves, it is the gift of God—*not by works, so that no one can boast*" (Eph. 2:8-9, emphasis added).

Meeting God is a free gift. You can't come to God based on your good works. Otherwise, you could boast, *I have a relationship with God because I'm such a good person.* The only reason any of us can meet God is not because we're such great people, but because He is such a great God. God, in love, offers us a gift—the gift of a friendship with Him, beginning the moment we place our faith in Christ's payment for our sins and enduring through all eternity.

But like any gift, you must accept it in order for the gift to be yours. Plenty of people are familiar with the concept of God's gift of forgiveness; lots of folks know about the gift of God's love; millions of women have heard about the gift of eternal life. Sadly, not everyone who knows about the gift of meeting God accepts the gift and makes it theirs.

Several years ago, long before iPods and iPads, when MP3 players were the newest and hottest gadget, JP bought me one for Christmas. I remember watching him as I opened his carefully selected present. The eager smile on his face told me he was excited about the gift and thought I would be too. I had never used an MP3 player and, frankly, I didn't really understand all the fuss about it. My life was just fine without one, thank you very much. Later that night, I tossed the MP3 in a drawer, where it gathered dust for over a year. One day, I stumbled onto the gift and decided to give it a try. The moment I placed the earphones into my ears I wondered why I had taken so long to unwrap the gift JP had so lovingly purchased for me.

Long ago, God purchased a gift for you that is infinitely more valuable than any technical gadget we might give one another. That gift—forgiveness for your sins, the certainty of heaven, eternal life, friendship with Almighty God—is yours if you take it. Don't let it sit in the drawer unwrapped. Reach out your hands, embrace Christ and meet God.

If this is the desire of your heart, take a moment right now and tell God. The prayer that follows isn't magic. God is concerned with your heart, not your words; but you may want to use this prayer as a springboard for your own.

> *Lord Jesus, I need You. I believe that You are the Son of God who died on the cross and rose again to pay the debt of my sin. Please forgive my sins. Come into my life. I want to know You as my God and my Lord. I want to follow You all the days of my life and be Your friend. Amen.*

The woman who knows Christ as her Savior knows God as her friend. You began reading this book seeking to meet God. The moment you come to believe and receive what Christ accomplished for you through His death and resurrection, the introduction is complete. The relationship begins. It's a relationship that lasts throughout this lifetime and throughout eternity. You can say with confidence, *God knows me, and I know God.*

Good news, indeed.

## For Further Study

What is one piece of good news you've received in the last 12 months?

In the Bible, the word "gospel" means "good news." Read Romans 1:14-16 and note:

How Paul felt about the gospel:

_____

_____

_____

Why he felt this way:

_____

_____

_____

_____

Complete this sentence: I am not ashamed of the gospel because it is _____ .

The good news of the gospel is that all people can be saved
from sin, from death, from judgment, from performance-ori-
ented religious works, from hypocrisy, from shame, from guilt,
from fear and from separation from God. In love, God reaches
down to save us because He has a purpose and plan for our
lives. Describe your reaction to this good news:

_____

_____

_____

_____

What is God's purpose and plan for you, according to the following verses?

John 3:16

_____

_____

_____

John 10:10

Romans 5:1

God wants all people to know Him. God's purpose and plan is that you would experience eternal life with Him in heaven, but also experience abundant life with Him now. If this is God's purpose and plan, why don't most people experience this plan?

Look up the following verses and note the problem faced by all people:

Isaiah 64:6

Jeremiah 17:9

Romans 3:10

Romans 3:23

What is the consequence of this problem?

Isaiah 59:2

Romans 6:23

Read Genesis 3:1-10. Before Adam and Eve chose to disobey God, they walked and talked with Him freely in the Garden of Eden.

According to verses 8-10, what did they do after they sinned?

According to verse 9, what did God do after they sinned?

What does God's response tell you about God's desire for relationship with man?

Based on the following verses, what is God's remedy for man's sin problem?

Romans 5:8

2 Corinthians 5:21

1 Peter 3:18

When I was in college, I had a friend who wondered why Jesus had to die on the cross. Wouldn't it have been enough for Christ to come to earth and live among us as an example? Death seemed so gruesome to her. Surely it wasn't necessary. Or was it? According to Romans 6:23, what is the price tag of sin?

Read Romans 5:6-10. Who paid the price for our sin?

Why?

_____

_____

_____

With what result?

_____

_____

What does the Bible say about Jesus being the one and only
way to God?

John 14:6

_____

_____

_____

Act 4:12

_____

_____

_____

1 Timothy 1:15

_____

_____

_____

1 John 5:12

_____

_____

_____

Look up Ephesians 2:8-9 and answer the following questions:

Can a person earn her way into heaven? Why or why not?

How is a person saved?

If a person offers you a gift, what must you do to receive it?

Entering into a relationship with God is a choice. God wants to meet you, but you must also want to meet Him. Jesus died to bridge the gap that separates sinful man from holy God. When a person accepts the gift of salvation by believing that Jesus died on the cross to pay the price tag for her sins, she becomes connected with God in a brand-new way. What God offers is not religion. God offers a relationship with Him through His Son, Jesus Christ.

Read the following verses and write down the phrase that indicates a choice, decision or action:

John 1:12

Acts 10:43

Romans 10:9-10

Romans 10:13

God offers the free gift of salvation to all who believe in Him and receive Him as their Savior and Lord. Do you believe that Jesus is who He claimed to be, and that He died on the cross for your sins and rose again? Would you like to receive His gift of salvation and have the assurance of eternal life?

If you answered yes to these questions, take a moment right now to talk to God. Remember, God isn't as interested in your words as He is with the attitude of your heart. All you must do is believe and call upon Him to save you. You may want to pray something like this:

> *Lord Jesus, I need You. I believe that You are the Son of God who died on the cross and rose again to pay the debt of my sin. Please forgive my sins. Come into my life. I want to know You as my God and my Lord. I want to follow You all the days of my life and be Your friend. Amen.*

# After the Introduction

If there's a single emotion that plagues virtually all women at some point in their life, it's got to be doubt. We doubt that we're good enough; that we're pretty enough; that we're smart enough; that we're loved enough. We doubt that our hopes and dreams will come true; that Mr. Right will ever come along; that we'll be happy if he doesn't. We doubt that we'll make right decisions. You name the issue, somehow doubt finds a way to creep in. Is it any wonder, then, that doubt slithers into our spiritual journey, making us question the reality of our salvation and security with God?

Most of us deal with doubt ineffectively. Some try to shove doubt aside, hoping it will disappear if left unattended. Others feed doubt with spiraling emotions and chaotic thoughts, only to find small doubts growing larger. Whatever our method of dealing with doubt, only one tactic silences it.

We must combat doubt with truth.

So, just exactly what *is* true about your relationship with God, once you decide to follow Christ? The truth is that your relationship with God is secure and can never to be severed. Nothing can separate you from the love of God. Nothing. Not you. Not your circumstances. Not your environment. Not your feelings. Not even the demons can unglue the love and commitment God has made to you, once you have entrusted your life to Him.

Your enemy, however, would like to make you think otherwise.

Jesus said, "The thief comes only to steal and kill and destroy; I have come that they may have life, and have it to the full" (John 10:10). Satan (the thief) doesn't want you to meet God, much less grow in your relationship with Him. He'll do everything in his power to rob you of your joy in your relationship with God, to kill your new commitment to Christ and destroy your faith.

Satan will prey on your doubt.

He may whisper thoughts like, *Are you sure you're really a Christian? You don't seem like one.* Or, *That Christianity stuff can't really be true, look at all the hypocrites.* Perhaps he'll try shaming you, casting doubt on God's unconditional love with ideas like, *God couldn't really forgive you after all you've done.* He might lure you into thinking, *God doesn't love women like you. You don't fit. Give it up.* Maybe he'll attempt to draw you away from God, enticing you with the lie that *life is so much more fun without God. Your life will be such a bore if you get religious.* Or perhaps he'll simply call into question your confidence, leaving you wondering if you somehow need to do more in order to really become a Christian.

Whatever the tactic, know this: Your enemy *will* try to cast doubt on your new relationship with God. Satan doesn't want you following God, any more than a Yankees fan wants someone to root for the Mets. Your enemy sees you as a defector. Once you were on his team; now you're on God's team. And he doesn't like it one bit.

If you've already experienced some of these doubts, you are experiencing what is known as "the spiritual battle." Every time a person tries to take a significant step toward God, the devil and his demons will try to pull her away. They're masters at using doubt, discouragement and temptation to prevent women like you and me from meeting and following God, which is why we must combat these lies with the truth.

# The Truth About Your New Relationship with God

The truth about your new relationship with God rests squarely on God's irrevocable Word. You don't have to rely on your feelings when it comes to being sure of your salvation. You wouldn't want to, anyway. Feelings make a faulty foundation for any relationship. Feelings can be as shifting as sand; one day you may feel close to God, the next day you may not feel close to God at all. Emotions cannot be the litmus test for the security of a believer. Instead, you must rely on what God says is true. Put your faith in the facts, and your feelings will follow.

---

WE MUST COMBAT DOUBT WITH TRUTH.

---

God's Word, in the book of 1 John, clarifies the facts surrounding your eternal security as a believer: "And this is the testimony: God has given us eternal life, and this life is in his Son. Whoever has the Son has life; whoever does not have the Son of God does not have life. I write these things to you who believe in the name of the Son of God so that you may *know* that you have eternal life" (1 John 5:11-13, emphasis added).

John makes it plain that whoever has God's Son has life; and whoever doesn't have the Son, doesn't have life. He penned these words to believers for a singular purpose: "So that you may know that you have eternal life." Not that "so you will hope you have eternal life" or "so you will cross your fingers and wish that you have eternal life" or "so that you will think positive thoughts to have eternal life." God's Word says, "so that you may *know* that you have eternal life." The Bible assures us of this: If we believe in the Son of God and have trusted Him as our Savior, we can know that we have eternal life.

Several weeks ago, JP and I attended an event where we waited to buy tickets at the door instead of purchasing them ahead of time. We'd done this many times before, so we didn't give it a second thought—until we arrived at the event and saw the line. Oops. JP and I exchanged glances. We knew our chances of getting in were iffy at best, so we took our place at the end of the line and crossed our fingers. As the line inched forward, we held our breath. It was going to be close. Finally, it was our turn. There were only a few tickets left, but enough for the two of us. Although we had been unsure we'd be allowed to enter only minutes before, once we had our tickets in hand it never crossed our minds that we might not be admitted. Our tickets, bought and paid for, served as our guarantee of entrance.

> PUT YOUR FAITH IN THE FACTS AND YOUR
> FEELINGS WILL FOLLOW.

In the same way, your sincere faith in what Christ did for you through His death and resurrection serves as your guarantee for admittance into heaven. Christ paid for your ticket. Your eternal destiny is secure. A person who relies on good works instead of Christ's payment for entrance into heaven is left wondering if she'll make it. But you don't have to wonder. You don't have to hope. You don't have to guess. You can know.

No matter what your doubt, this is truth.

## Nothing Can Make God *Not* Love You

Because your security with God is based on what God has done for you, it's also true that nothing can separate you from God's love. The apostle Paul explains:

If God is for us, who can ever be against us? Since he did not spare even his own Son but gave him up for us all, won't he also give us everything else? . . . Can anything ever separate us from Christ's love? Does it mean he no longer loves us if we have trouble or calamity, or are persecuted, or hungry, or destitute, or in danger, or threatened with death? . . . No, despite all these things, overwhelming victory is ours through Christ, who loved us. And I am convinced that nothing can ever separate us from God's love. Neither death nor life, neither angels nor demons, neither our fears for today nor our worries about tomorrow—not even the powers of hell can separate us from God's love. No power in the sky above or in the earth below—indeed, nothing in all creation will ever be able to separate us from the love of God that is revealed in Christ Jesus our Lord (Rom. 8:31-32,35,37-39, *NLT*).

God is for you.

*God* is for *you*.

God has already given you His very best—His very own Son; therefore, He can be trusted to give you everything else you need, including eternal life with Him. Picture a loved one giving you $50,000. After giving you a gift as generous as this, do you think that person would hesitate to buy you a cup of coffee? Of course not! That's the picture created in Romans 8. If the God of the universe didn't spare His Son for you, He'll surely take care of you.

What's more, God doesn't accuse or condemn you. Ever. Many women aren't familiar with this kind of unconditional love and commitment. Maybe you're one of them. We tend to think of God in light of our human experiences. In our world, loved ones leave, friends let us down, parents shame, and co-workers betray. It's almost mind-boggling to consider a God who will never leave us, who will never forsake us. It can be hard to wrap our minds around a God who defends us; a God who won't condemn us; a God who loves us no matter what. How can this possibly be true? Based on what Jesus did for you and me through His death and resurrection, God is the one who has given us right standing with Himself. The moment we trust Christ as our Savior, God declares us righteous, not because we are perfect, but because He is perfect. God's love isn't based on our performance, but on His; therefore, His love for us cannot be broken, stolen or severed.

What about our struggles, our hardships, our bad breaks? Do those things mean God doesn't love us? Not at all. Though our enemy may try to lure us into believing our trials and difficulties mean that God has turned His back on us, the Bible makes it clear that even in these situations we can be conquerors through Christ. Jesus told His followers plainly, "In this world you will have trouble. But take heart! I have overcome the world" (John 16:33). God walks with us through our pain and adversity. We don't have to face life's trials and difficulties alone, as we did before we met God. Like a child who clings tightly to her father's hand, we can rest securely in God's care. God sustains us when we have depleted every last ounce of strength we possess. When we are weak, He is strong. God assures us that we can cast all our cares upon Him, because He cares for us (see 1 Pet. 5:7).

Satan wants you to believe otherwise. He'll try to get you to buy into the notion that if you were *really* a Christian, or if God *really* existed, or if God *really* loved you as much as the gal down the street, your hardships, heartaches and difficulties would vanish into thin air. Better yet, they would never materialize in the first place. He'll prey on your fragile emotions to tempt you to doubt God's love and goodness, if he can. Don't forget that he comes only to steal, kill and destroy. He's the father of lies.

God walks by your side all day, every day. "I am always with you; you hold me by my right hand" (Ps. 73:23). Nothing—*nothing*—can separate you from God's love for you. This isn't a feel-good platitude or wishful thinking. This is the truth. This truth gives you assurance and quenches your doubts. This is truth with which you can extinguish the fiery darts of doubt that Satan throws your way.

## Safe in the Palm of His Hand

The moment you become a follower of Christ, God secures your eternal destiny. The woman who has the Son has eternal life. She also has the unbreakable, unconditional love of God. Jesus explained the bond between a believer and Himself this way: "My sheep listen to my voice; I know them, and they follow me. I give them eternal life, and they shall never perish; no one will snatch them out of my hand" (John 10:27-28).

Reread the last line. Who can snatch you out of Jesus' hand? Who can rob you of your security in Christ? Who can take away your eternal destiny? Who can cause you to lose your salvation? No one.

No one, and no thing.

When our children were toddlers, occasionally they would find a treasure they refused to part with. These "treasures" ran the spectrum from small bugs, to tiny kid's meal toys, to pieces of candy. Committed to keeping their beloved item, they would wrap tiny fingers tightly around the object, sometimes holding on so fiercely that JP or I would have to pry their fingers off the object. However, no matter how tightly they held on to their treasure, we managed to take it away because we were bigger, stronger and more powerful.

No one, however, can snatch away a treasure that God has placed firmly in His hand. When you become a Christian, God places you in the palm of His hand, wraps His sovereign fingers around your life and continues to hold on tight. No one can pry open His divine fingers, because no being is bigger or stronger or more powerful than our Almighty Creator. Nothing can snatch you out of His hand. You cannot lose your salvation. Your relationship with God is secure.

When doubts plague your mind, remember what is truth.

## Experiencing the Assurance of Your Relationship with God

The Bible is filled with objective truth statements about the assurance of a believer's relationship with God. Objective reality remains true despite fluctuations of feelings. If something is true, it remains true, whether we feel like it is or not; whether we believe it or not; whether we understand it or not. Truth does not change. The more we focus on the truth, the more doubts will fade. We combat doubt with truth.

However, in addition to objective assurance of salvation, we can also subjectively experience the assurance of our relationship with God. While objective assurance depends upon the promises made in God's Word, subjective assurance depends upon our obedience to God's Word. As you begin to see your life change, becoming more in line with the character of Christ, your heart is reassured of the authenticity of your faith.

The moment a woman becomes a Christian, she becomes a brand-new person. "If anyone is in Christ, the new creation has come: The old has gone, the new is here!" (2 Cor. 5:17). Because

God gives His Holy Spirit to dwell in believers, you will begin to notice a hunger for God and His ways. The more you understand the depth of God's love for you, the more you'll want to please Him. The book of 1 John explains it this way:

> We know that we have come to know him if we keep his commands. Whoever says, "I know him," but does not do what he commands is a liar, and the truth is not in that person. But if anyone obeys his word, love for God is truly made complete in them. *This is how we know we are in him* (1 John 2:3-5, emphasis added).

There is an inseparable link between knowing God and obeying God. If a woman truly believes, she obeys. It's that simple. Does she obey perfectly? No. Perfection doesn't happen until heaven, but her life will show evidence of her faith. It's this progressive life transformation that gives us confidence and assurance of our faith. The word "know" refers to personal, experiential knowledge. In other words, our obedience to Christ provides us with personal confidence in the authenticity of our relationship with God. As we see our life transform and our faith grow, we experience what God says is true about the reality of our new connection with Him. The truth always remains true, but our obedience to the truth enables us to experience it.

Not long ago, I had a conversation with a woman who had recently become a Christian. She candidly told me she was praying about something rather personal, something she would never have considered praying about before she met God. This piqued my interest. She went on to reveal that she had a neighbor that she really, *really* didn't like. Pretty much hated her, in fact. But since she'd become a Christian, she realized her feelings weren't okay. Her new understanding of God's unconditional love ignited a desire to love others. Even her neighbor. So she began praying that God would help her to love her neighbor.

What would motivate a woman to pray for help in changing her attitude toward someone she could probably more easily avoid? Only an authentic relationship with God. Her sensitivity and obedience to God serve as evidence of her new life in Christ.

---

IF WE KNOW GOD AND LOVE HIM, WE WILL SEEK TO REFLECT GOD BY OBEYING HIM.

---

Marks of faith have been worn throughout history by virtually all world religions. Muslim women wear face veils. Jewish men wear yarmulkes. Hindus place a *bindi*, or dot, on their foreheads. Sikhs don turbans. These symbols are meant to be outward expressions of faith. However, the mark—the symbol—that sets apart a Christian is love. Jesus told His followers quite clearly that the mark of a Christian is love. "A new command I give you: Love one another. As I have loved you, so you must love one another. By this everyone will know that you are my disciples, if you love one another" (John 13:34-35). God is love. When we love others, we not only please God by obeying His instruction, but we also live freely in the security that we have, in fact, met God. Love is the singular mark of authentic faith in Christ. When God's love fills our hearts, that love expresses itself to those around us, and we experience the assurance of our salvation.

If we know God and love Him, we will seek to reflect God by obeying Him. Our obedience authenticates our profession of faith. A person isn't a Christian just because he or she says words like, "I believe in God" or "Christ died for my sins" or "I've been saved." These are meaningless phrases unless they are backed up by a desire to follow in the footsteps of Christ. We won't do it perfectly. We will do it much like a child learning to walk; we learn to walk with God a step at a time. Sometimes we may falter. Sometimes we may fall. Occasionally, we may even run in the wrong direction. Falls and failures aren't fatal in the Christian life if we learn from our mistakes, turn from our disobedience and start walking in step with Christ once again. Just as our obedience gives us experiential proof of our faith, so does our repentance. The most prominent and important sign of authentic Christianity, however, is love.

---

FALLS AND FAILURES AREN'T FATAL IN THE CHRISTIAN LIFE IF WE LEARN FROM OUR MISTAKES, TURN FROM OUR DISOBEDIENCE AND START WALKING IN STEP WITH CHRIST ONCE AGAIN.

---

## Assurance in a Nutshell

Every woman deals with doubt over something, at least occasionally; but doubt about your relationship with God doesn't need to plague you if you've trusted Christ for you salvation. The security that comes from a relationship with God through Jesus Christ is both objective and subjective. Objectively, we rely on the truth of God's Word regarding the assurance of our salvation, rather than the fickleness of our feelings. Subjectively, our increasing obedience confirms in our own minds and hearts that we are, in fact, true followers of Christ. We won't always *feel* like we have authentic faith. We won't always act like it, either, though we will see progress. But we can be assured of our relationship with God by trusting what He says in His Word.

These things I have written to you so that you may *know* that you have eternal life.

# For Further Study

Read 1 John 5:11-13 and answer the following questions:

Who gives eternal life?

In whom is eternal life found?

Who has eternal life?

Who does not have eternal life?

Why did John say he wrote these things?

If you have sincerely prayed to accept Christ Jesus as your Savior, several things are now true about you. According to the verses listed below, what are they?

John 10:28

John 15:14-15

2 Corinthians 5:17

Galatians 2:20

Ephesians 1:13-14

Philippians 1:6

Romans 5:1

Romans 8:1

Romans 8:38-39

Hebrews 7:25

Hebrews 13:5 and Deuteronomy 31:6

Which of these truths are most meaningful to you? Why?

Which of these truths are hardest for you to embrace as true?

What impact will these truths have upon your confidence in your relationship with God?

Read the following verses and note what character quality distinguishes someone who possesses authentic faith:

John 13:34-35

1 John 4:7-12

According to the verses listed below, what is the relationship between knowing God and obeying God?

Deuteronomy 11:1

_____

_____

_____

John 14:23

_____

_____

_____

1 John 2:3-5

_____

_____

_____

If you are doing this study in a group, ask a group member to pray for you this week. If you are doing the study alone, take a moment right now and thank God for all the blessings that are yours, now that you are a child of God.

# Growing to Know the God You Seek

Have you ever wondered why some people have a close, intimate, life-giving relationship with God, and others do not? Have you ever considered why some Christians radiate God's love, joy and peace, and other Christians seem harsh, negative and burdened? Ever asked yourself why you can see the love of Christ in one person's facial expressions, or in the way she handles life's hardships, or in the way she treats other people? Or why one woman continues to grow in her love, knowledge and obedience to Christ, and another woman falters? How come one believer's faith flourishes and another believer's faith stagnates?

The answer is simple, really. We grow in our relationship with God to the degree that we cultivate our relationship with God.

I love flowers. Nothing makes me happier than looking out my kitchen window onto a view of healthy, vibrant blossoms lining the flower beds and pots in my backyard. Over the years, I have spent hundreds of dollars on plants, flowers and shrubs. Sadly, not all of those plants have lived. I've watched far too many waste away due to overwatering, under-watering or a combination of both. Although I love flowers, I don't have a green thumb. Not even light green. Caring for plants doesn't come naturally to me. In fact, during one 12-month period, I killed every single topiary houseplant I owned. That is, until a girlfriend gave me the secret to their care: "Water with one ice cube every day and you'll never give them too much to drink or too little." With that one piece of knowledge I've been able to keep a variety of houseplants alive and thriving for years. Consider this chapter your "one ice cube a day" secret to spiritual growth.

Essentially, the secret for growth involves cultivating your relationship with God in four ways: through God's Word; through relationship with other believers; through prayer and worship; and through service. These four elements keep us connected to God.

## Stay Connected to Christ

Jesus must have liked plants, too, because He used an enlightening horticultural illustration to explain how Christians grow and flourish. Passing by a grape vine, Jesus paused to point out the connection between the vine and its branches: "I am the vine; you are the branches. If you remain in me and I in you, you will bear much fruit; apart from me you can do nothing" (John 15:5). Just as a branch must stay connected to the vine in order to produce fruit, so must we stay connected to Christ to bear spiritual fruit.

Jesus explained that connection to Him was the key to spiritual growth. A person cannot be a growing, fruitful Christian without maintaining her connection to Christ; that's what Jesus meant when He said, "apart from me you can do nothing." If you cultivate your spiritual life by talking to God, allowing God to talk to you, obeying what He says and becoming connected with other believers, your relationship with God will thrive and grow.

# Know and Follow God's Word

When Moses (the guy who led the Israelites across the Red Sea after God parted it) died, and his protégé, Joshua, assumed leadership over the nation of Israel, God gave him a single piece of instruction—the secret of spiritual success, really:

> Be strong and very courageous. Be careful to obey all the law my servant Moses gave you; do not turn from it to the right or to the left, that you may be successful wherever you go. Keep this Book of the Law always on your lips; meditate on it day and night, so that you may be careful to do everything written in it. Then you will be prosperous and successful. Have I not commanded you? Be strong and courageous. Do not be afraid; do not be discouraged, for the LORD your God will be with you wherever you go (Josh. 1:7-9).

God knew that Joshua had a big task ahead of him. Providing military, spiritual and political leadership to over 2 million people would be no picnic in the park. To assure Joshua's fruitful leadership, God commanded him to be strong and courageous, being careful to know and obey God's Word. If Joshua did these things, he would prosper and succeed.

In the same way, growing spiritually takes strength and courage. When we immerse ourselves in God's Word, the Bible, learning it and obeying it as we travel through life, we too can be fruitful and successful in our walk with God. Like Joshua, we must make sure that God's Word doesn't depart from us.

The more we get into God's Word, the more God's Word gets into us. The more we immerse ourselves in God's Word, the more connected we stay to Christ. The more God's Word weaves itself into the fabric of our lives, the more fruitful our lives become. It's that simple.

Timothy's mentor, the apostle Paul, wanted Timothy to grasp the importance of God's Word in the life of a believer. In a letter to Timothy, Paul wrote, "All Scripture is God-breathed and is useful for teaching, rebuking, correcting and training in righteousness" (2 Tim. 3:16). In other words, the Bible is God's personal message to us. As such, the words of the Bible teach us truth about right and wrong, about God and His love, about spiritual life and growth, and about God's eternal plans. God's Word is the single greatest teacher for our spiritual growth.

As all good teachers know, true learning comes not merely from knowing content, but from applying it. That's where the benefit of rebuke and correction comes in. The Bible helps us grow by pointing out where we fall short. It corrects us by giving us ways to live rightly, rather than in disobedience. It trains us, helping us to continually grow in our faith. Promises, encouragement and stories of hope and redemption fill the pages of Scripture, opening our eyes to God's work in our lives and our circumstances. God's Word, the Bible, teaches us, rebukes us, corrects us and trains us. All Scripture—every word—profits you and me in some way, which is why it's vital that we know it and obey it.

Because knowing and applying God's Word is central to our spiritual growth, we must read it regularly. Generally, the best place for a new believer to start reading the Bible is with the book of John, which is the fourth book of the New Testament. John's gospel provides an eyewitness account of Jesus' life and covers most of the major Christian doctrines essential to faith. This book of the Bible contains 21 chapters; so if you read one chapter a day (which will take only about 5 to 10 minutes), you'll have completed the book in three weeks. After reading the book of John, try reading Ephesians, Philippians or Colossians, which are all books chock-full of instructions on how to live as a follower of Christ. Then tackle the book of Romans, which explains the major tenets of the Christian faith.

Before I read my Bible each day, I say a simple prayer: "Lord, if You were here with me right now (and You are!), what would You say to me today?" Reading the Bible is reading God's love letter to you. When you read it, God wants to speak to you. He has something He wants you to know, feel or do. (Seriously, isn't that kind of mind-blowing?!) Ask God to speak to you through the time you spend reading His Word, and watch how your understanding and love for God grow.

Further your knowledge of God's Word by joining a Bible study. Find a church where God's Word is taught each Sunday and attend regularly. Memorize verses to help you grow in your faith. Listen to podcasts of sermons or Scripture. The apostle Peter wrote, "Like newborn babies, crave spiritual milk, so that by it you may grow up in your salvation" (1 Pet. 2:2). In many ways, a new believer is a "baby" Christian who requires frequent nourishment of God's Word in order to thrive.

WE GROW IN OUR RELATIONSHIP WITH
GOD TO THE DEGREE THAT WE CULTIVATE
OUR RELATIONSHIP WITH GOD.

If you've ever experienced a "sugar low," you're familiar with that listless, no-energy-to-do-anything feeling that washes over you when you've gone too long between meals. Some Christians suffer from a "spiritual low" because they fail to spiritually feed themselves on a regular basis. The result is a lackluster spiritual experience void of energy and passion for God. Don't let that be you. Allow God to feed your soul through His Word. Just as your body needs physical food to stay healthy, so too your soul needs spiritual food. You can't go for days on end without physical food and thrive; neither can you go for days on end without spiritual food. Feed yourself on God's Word every day.

## Get Connected with Other Christians

God uses His Word to renew our mind, transform our life and help us grow. God also uses His people. In fact, when we place our faith in Christ, not only do we begin a new relationship with Him, but we also begin a new relationship with other believers. We are brought into the family of God, sometimes called "the Body of Christ" or "the Church." The word "church" refers not only to a local congregation of believers, but also to every believer, in every place, in every time. The "Church" is comprised of all people who place their faith in Jesus Christ for the forgiveness of their sins, irrespective of what label might be found above their church door. To grow in our relationship with God, we need other believers, and they need us.

When our youngest daughter was six, she attended a birthday party at a local mini-amusement park. You know the kind—the ones with miniature golf, arcade games, rock-climbing walls, and so on. The girls ended their day driving miniature racecars. Unlike the cars at Disneyland or Disneyworld, these cars were not on tracks. Instead, each child was expected to drive her own vehicle. Entertaining, to say the least.

I watched from the sidelines as Ashton giddily stepped into her car, fastened her seatbelt and waited for the flag signal to start. Finally, the flag was lowered and the girls were off. Ashton floored her accelerator as she flew around the track. I distinctly remember thinking, *Thank goodness she doesn't get her driver's license for another 10 years.* The kid was a maniac.

In fact, Ashton was so out of control that she hit everything in her path—the other cars, the guardrail—everything. The child couldn't stay straight to save her life.

Unless . . .

As I continued to watch Ashton, I began to notice a pattern. The only time she didn't swerve was if—and only if—she had a driver on her right and a driver on her left, quite literally bumping her into place. As long as Ashton remained sandwiched between two more experienced drivers, she drove straight. Remove just one of the protective cars, however, and she swerved all over the raceway.

You and I are like Ashton on that racetrack.

Left to our own devices, we can all too easily swerve all over the path of life. And it doesn't take much to get us swerving, does it? One bad-hair day; one piece of bad news; one relational conflict; one seemingly insurmountable problem; one alluring temptation; one financial setback. Throw just one of these issues onto our path, and we can find ourselves swerving emotionally, physically or spiritually. We *need* godly people surrounding us, aiding us to stay the course on our Christian journey.

We are told in Hebrews 10:23 to "hold unswervingly to the hope we profess." How can we hold unswervingly to our hope in Christ? By making sure we surround ourselves with Christian friends, mentors and teachers who will support us in our journey of faith. Does this mean we need to abandon our non-believing friends, family and co-workers? No. Not at all. (Unless, of course, these relationships are destructive to our spiritual, emotional or physical wellbeing.) But under normal conditions, surrounding ourselves with believers who will help keep us bumped into place simply means we need to add strong Christian connections into our relationship mix.

Practically speaking, how can you do this? Find a small group or Bible study and go weekly. Attend church every week, but don't just sit there and then scram as soon as it's over. Stick around to meet people. Find a place to serve alongside other believers. Ask God to bring Christian friends into your life.

The summer between our middle daughter's sophomore and junior years in high school, she and I began praying that she would connect with at least one strong Christian friend. Each night I made my way into the darkness of her bedroom, kissed her goodnight and prayed the same words: "Lord, please bring Kylie strong Christian girlfriends who are really fun too." What Kylie needed then, you need now. Whether you are 16 or 60, strong, supportive Christian friends are essential for spiritual growth. And hey, our friends need to be fun too!

If you're lacking a solid Christian support system, ask God to bring people into your life to help you as you learn to walk with Him. Pray for positive Christian relationships, then keep your eyes open as you seek out people who will help you hold unswervingly to the hope you profess.

## Find a Place to Serve

Being part of a local body of believers where the Bible is taught and where you can find encouragement and accountability is vital to your Christian growth, but that's just the start. The moment you trust Christ as your Savior, you are given a spiritual gift that makes you an integral part of the Body of Christ. Your gift is more than a talent; it is a unique skill set God has given to you for the express purpose of helping others to grow in their relationship with Him. Each believer is to serve the other members of God's family so that each of us can continue to grow in our knowledge and love of Christ.

The Bible mentions 20 distinct spiritual gifts. When a woman places her faith in Christ, God gifts her uniquely for His service. Essentially, spiritual gifts are divided into either speaking gifts (like the gift of teaching, encouragement or words of wisdom) or serving gifts (mercy, giving, leadership, administration or hospitality, for example). As you grow in your relationship with God, discover your unique giftedness and use your gifts to serve those around you. As you serve others, you serve Christ, and your love for God and relationship with Him will grow and flourish.

## Talk to God Daily

If you talk to anyone with a successful marriage or long-term friendship, you'll find that his or her secret of success has something to do with staying connected throughout the changing seasons of life. What's true for a healthy marriage or lifelong friendship holds true for a healthy lifelong relationship with God. To grow in your relationship with God, you must stay connected to God. Just as a married couple needs to talk regularly in order to stay in love, so too must we connect with God by talking to Him in prayer.

You can talk to God anytime, anyplace, about anything.

In fact, the Bible gives us this encouragement: "The Lord is near. Do not be anxious about anything, but in every situation, by prayer and petition, with thanksgiving, present your requests to God" (Phil. 4:5-6). When we bring the totality of our life to God in prayer—our victories and defeats, our joys and sorrows, our worries and worship—an exchange takes place. We swap our limited perspective for God's sovereign one. We trade our hopelessness for His help. We substitute our weakness with His worship. And we are changed. We grow. We love and know God more as we see Him work in us and through us in response to our prayers.

How can you cultivate your prayer life? First, decide to talk to God every day. Before your head hits the pillow at night, ask yourself, *Did I talk to God today?* If not, take a few minutes to tell Him what's on your heart. Thank Him for your day and for your blessings. Worship Him for who He is and what He has done, and is doing, in your life.

To aid my prayer life, I write down my prayers. This isn't a list. Nor is it a journal about what happened in my day. It's a messy, private, written conversation with God. I write out my prayers longhand for two reasons: First, it serves as a reminder about what I've prayed and how God responded. Second, and perhaps more importantly, writing my prayers helps keep my mind focused. Although I have the best of intentions when it comes to prayer, I often find that about two nanoseconds after I've said "dear Lord" my mind wanders onto thoughts of work, errands, family, you name it. I find that when I write down my prayers, my mind and heart stay focused on my conversation with God. If you're like me, try writing down your prayers—your conversations—with God.

Praying out loud also helps me stay focused in prayer. In fact, I find that the prayers I speak feel more powerful than the prayers I say silently in my mind. Try turning off the radio while you're driving and talk with God instead. Use your time alone to connect with Christ by talking with Him about your life, just as you would talk with a friend. Thank God for all He's doing in your life. Praise Him for His goodness and character. Talk to Him about your loved ones and their concerns. Ask Him to give you wisdom and direct your path.

Talking with God keeps us connected with God. When we stay connected with God, we're like a branch that draws its resources from the vine. We become fruitful and productive. We grow.

Like a healthy plant, a solid marriage or a longtime friendship, our relationship with God must be cultivated and nurtured in order to thrive and develop. Practice the spiritual habits of reading God's Word daily; regularly connecting with growing Christians; serving others; praying about everything. If you do, your love and knowledge of God will increase.

## The Secret to Spiritual Growth in a Word

If you were to peek inside my Bible, you would see many verses underlined. One Scripture, however, holds a special place in my heart. If one verse could define my life, perhaps this verse would be it:

> My heart has heard you say, "Come and talk with me." And my heart responds, "LORD, I am coming" (Ps. 27:8, *NLT*).

Many, many years have come and gone since I was the 10-year-old girl perched in the backseat of my parents' station wagon, head filled full of questions about God. Like all of us, I had doubts. I had concerns. I had issues. But in spite of the questions—or maybe because of them—I decided to seek. My heart heard God say, "Come and talk with Me." So I did. What began as a season of seeking answers to my questions about God ended up as a way of life in relating to God.

Seeking God isn't something that you do only when you are exploring the possibility of meeting Him. Seeking God is something you continue to do in order to know Him, love Him and follow Him. Seeking God is both the gateway to meet God and the pathway to grow in your relationship with Him.

Continue to seek and you will find.

You will seek me and find me when you seek me with all your heart (Jer. 29:13).

## For Further Study

In John 15, Jesus compares our relationship with God to one of a vine and a branch. Read John 15:4-5.

What does Jesus tell us to do?

With what result?

What will happen if we don't stay connected to Christ?

According to John 15:9-11, how do we stay connected to Christ?

According to Joshua 1:7-9, the Word of God helps us to be prosperous (or fruitful) in our relationship with God. List the ways you are to incorporate God's laws into your life.

You get God's Word into your life in six ways:

1. Reading it
2. Listening to it
3. Studying it
4. Meditating on it
5. Memorizing it
6. Applying it

Write down one way you will get God's Word into your life every day this week. Share with your group.

How does God's Word help to transform you?

Romans 12:2

Romans 15:4

1 Peter 2:2

1 Peter 3:17

How does God use other believers to encourage us in our walk with Him?

Romans 1:11

2 Corinthians 13:11

Ephesians 4:15-17

Colossians 2:1-3

Hebrews 10:23-25

How has God used another person to encourage you in your relationship with Him? Be as specific as possible.

Some people contend that since their faith is a personal matter, they don't need to be part of a church. Based on the Scriptures above, how would you answer this objection?

Jesus warns us about the importance of correct doctrine and personal accountability to ensure that our faith remains growing and strong. Read Matthew 24:11-13. What is Jesus' warning?

Read the following passages and list all the spiritual gifts mentioned:

Romans 12:3-8

1 Corinthians 12:4-11

Read 1 Corinthians 12:11-31.

Who gives spiritual gifts?

Why are the gifts given?

Are some gifts better than others? What does this passage of Scripture tell us about each gift?

According to 1 Corinthians 13:1-3, what is the most important thing to keep in mind when using your spiritual gift?

How can you begin serving other people in Jesus' name?

What is easiest for you—being in God's Word, gathering with God's people, or serving others in God's name? Which is most challenging?

If you are doing this study in a group, ask one person to pray for you this week regarding the area in which you find the most challenge to your spiritual growth.

# The Books of the Bible

## Old Testament

| | | |
|---|---|---|
| Genesis | Hosea | |
| Exodus | Joel | |
| Leviticus | Amos | |
| Numbers | Obadiah | |
| Deuteronomy | Jonah | |
| Joshua | Micah | |
| Judges | Nahum | |
| Ruth | Habakkuk | |
| 1 Samuel | Zephaniah | |
| 2 Samuel | Haggai | |
| 1 Kings | Zechariah | |
| 2 Kings | Malachi | |
| 1 Chronicles | | |
| 2 Chronicles | | |
| Ezra | | |
| Nehemiah | | |
| Esther | | |
| Job | | |
| Psalms | | |
| Proverbs | | |
| Ecclesiastes | | |
| Song of Solomon | | |
| Isaiah | | |
| Jeremiah | | |
| Lamentations | | |
| Ezekiel | | |
| Daniel | | |

## New Testament

Matthew
Mark
Luke
John
Acts
Romans
1 Corinthians
2 Corinthians
Galatians
Ephesians
Philippians
Colossians
1 Thessalonians
2 Thessalonians
1 Timothy
2 Timothy
Titus
Philemon
Hebrews
James
1 Peter
2 Peter
1 John
2 John
3 John
Jude
Revelation

# Bibliography

James, R. *Thirsty*. Orlando, FL: CruPress, 2009.

Jones, D. C. "The Bibliographical Test Updated," *Christian Research Journal*, 2012.

Lewis, C. S. *Mere Christianity*. New York: Macmillan/Collier, 1955.

McDowell, J. *More Than a Carpenter*. Carol Stream, IL: Tyndale House, 1977.

———. *The New Evidence that Demands a Verdict*. Nashville, TN: Thomas Nelson, 1999.

Metzger, Bruce M. and Bart D. Ehrman. *The Text of the New Testament; Its Transmission, Corruption, and Restoration*. New York: Oxford University Press, 2005.

Visit

## Donna

at

## donnajones.org

Find companion resources for *Seek*, including
free downloads, videos, and
the Bible study leadership guide.

. . . . . . . . . . . .

Or book Donna to speak for your group or event.

# YES!

## Your child is just weeks away from good manners!

Think it's an impossible dream? Think again. Whether you're training your two-year-old to say "please" or talking with your teenager about how to treat others, you can have a well-mannered child in six weeks or less.